ESSAYS
IN
NATIONAL IDEALISM

ESSAYS
IN
NATIONAL IDEALISM

BY
ANANDA K. COOMARASWAMY

GYAN

Published by

GYAN

Gyan Publishing House
5, Ansari Road
Daryaganj, New Delhi-110002
Phone: 011-47034999, 9811692060
E-mail: books@gyanbooks.com

Distribution Network
gyanbooks.com
India, USA, Canada, UK, Australia, France

ISBN: 978-81-212-8340-3 (PB)
First Published, 1909

2nd Impression 2023

Printed at: Gyan Press, Delhi.

ESSAYS IN NATIONAL IDEALISM
Author: ANANDA K. COOMARASWAMY

ESSAYS IN NATIONAL IDEALISM: BY ANANDA K. COOMARASWAMY, D.Sc.

ESSAYS

IN

NATIONAL IDEALISM.

BY

ANANDA K. COOMARASWAMY.

PAGE.

ERRATA.

p. 43, 1.3; after *of* read *by such writers as being.*
p. 56, 1.27, for *or* read *on.*
p. 180, 1.1, for *item* read *time.*

POSTSCRIPT. Many of the chapters in this book are reprinted by permission from the *Modern Review*, the *Hindustan Review*, the *Indian Review*, and *Orpheus*, with additions and revision.

" Fair were my fate, beloved, if I be yet on the earth,
When the world is awaken at last, and from mouth to mouth they tell
Of thy love and thy deeds and thy valour, and thy hope that nought can quell."*

* "*The Pilgrims of Hope.*" *By William Morris.*

PREFACE.

THESE essays represent an endeavour towards an explanation of the true significance of the national movement in India. This movement can only be rightly understood, and has ultimate importance only, as an idealistic movement. Its outward manifestations have attracted abundant notice; the deeper meaning of the struggle is sometimes forgotten, alike in England and in India. Were this meaning understood, I believe that not only the world at large, but a large part even of the English people, would extend to India a true sympathy in her life and death struggle with an alien bureaucracy. For this struggle is much more than a political conflict. It is a struggle for spiritual and mental freedom from the domination of an alien ideal. In such a conflict, political and economic victory are but half the battle; for an India "free in name, but subdued by Europe in her inmost soul" would ill justify the price of freedom. It is not so much the material, as the moral and spiritual, subjection of Indian civilisation that in the end impoverishes humanity.

William Morris wrote some twenty-seven years ago concerning Socialism,—and few have worked more whole-heartedly for a cause than he did for the ideal that he understood by Socialism,— "Meantime I can see no use in people having political freedom unless they use it as an instrument for leading reasonable and manlike lives; no good even in education if; when they are educated, people have only slavish work to do, and have to live lives too much beset with sordid anxiety for them to be able to think and feel with the more fortunate people who produced art and poetry and great thought."

To a few it may appear strange that in a book devoted to the ends of Indian nationalism, so much space should be given to art, so little said of politics. It is because nations are made by artists and by poets, not by traders and politicians. Art contains in itself the deepest principles of life, the truest guide to the greatest art, the Art of Living. The true life, the ideal of Indian culture, is itself a unity and an art, because of its inspiration by one ruling passion, the desire to realise a spiritual inheritance. All things in India have been valued in the light of this desire. No other ideal can ever ultimately shape or determine the Indian character. In the immediate future this passion for self-sacrifice and self-realisation will find expression in a nationalism which will be essentially religious in its sanction. Thus once more by the inspiration of a ruling passion—the religious and national ideal in one—the Art of Life will be realised again; only by thus becoming artists and poets, can we again understand our own art and poetry, and thereby attain the highest ideal of nationality, the will and the power to give.

Something of this kind is the burden of my essays,—that we should endeavour more to be great than to possess great things. All honour to those who have spent their lives in the political struggle; yet I believe that it is not through politics that revolutions are made, and that National Unity needs a deeper foundation than the perception of political wrongs. The true Nationalist is an Idealist; and for him that deeper cause of the Unrest is the longing for Self-realisation. He realises that Nationalism is a duty even more than a right; and that the duty of upholding the national Dharma is incompatible with intellectual slavery, and therefore he seeks to free himself, and through others like himself, his country.

It is possible to find in true art not merely the spiritual, but, or rather therefore, the material regeneration of India. The educated Indian of to-day, says a sympathetic writer, is behind the rest of the world in artistic understanding. Few have realised in how far the inefficiency and poverty of modern India is the direct result of this. Contrast Japan.

Japan is to a large degree living upon the strength of her past. That strength lies far more than we suspect, in her art:

> "To many persons it may appear incredible that the consistence of Japan's statesmanship and strategy, the far reach of her military plans, the splendid qualities of her soldiers and sailors, the steadiness of nerve, the accuracy of aim, the coolness of advance, the deadliness of attack, the self-immolation of regiments at the word of command, are not unconnected with the fact that she alone among living nations has a truly national art, that her senses are refined and her taste fastidious, that her poor love beauty and seek their pleasure amongst flowers. This is a hard saying, but the truth is even so." *

The causes which have led to the degeneration of Indian art, and prevent its revival, are identical with those that prevent the recovery of her political efficiency.

I do not believe in any regeneration of the Indian people which cannot find expression in art; any reawakening worth the name *must* so express itself. There can be no true realisation of political unity until Indian life is again inspired by the unity of the national culture. More necessary, therefore, than all the labours of politicians, is National Education. We should not rest satisfied until the entire control of Indian education is in Indian hands. It is a matter in which no European should have a voice, save by the express invitation of Indians. For

* Hibbert Journal, October, 1905.

those only can educate who sympathise. Every Government and missionary college and school must be replaced by colleges and schools of our own, where young men and women are taught to be true Indians. So long as Indians are prepared to accept an education the aim of which is to make them English in all but colour—and at present they do in the main accept such education—they cannot achieve a national unity.

An India united by even one generation of National Education would not need to ask or fight for freedom. It would be hers in fact, for none could resist that united aloofness of spirit which could make the mental atmosphere of India unbreathable by any but friends. The vital forces associated with the national movement in India are not merely political, but moral, literary, and artistic; and their significance lies in the fact that India henceforth will, in the main, judge all things by her own standards and from her own point of view. But the two sides of the national movement, the material and the spiritual, are inseparable, and must attain success or fail together. Political freedom and full responsibility are essential to self-respect and self-development. Believing this, it will be understood how impossible it is that any supposed or real advantages resulting from the British dominion in India could ever lead us to accept the indefinite continuance of that dominion as part of our ideal. Granting the reality of some of these advantages—and no-one would pretend that the Government of India by England has been an absolutely unmixed evil—the fact remains that we in India hold the price of any such advantages to be too high. In the words of Thoreau, the cost of a thing is the whole amount of what may be called life, which has to be exchanged for it, immediately, or in the long run. The advantages, such as they may be, are outweighed by the paralysis of the live moral forces of the nation, resulting from the removal of responsibility.

It is a paradox to speak of preparing a people for self-government. Alien government, by removing responsibility, and the natural motives for public spirit, tends only to unfit a subject people for independent action. The chief lessons in self-government which England has given to India, have been given in the last few years; given however, not in the officially controlled municipalities and universities, but in the necessity which the present situation has revealed to the Indian people,—the necessity for unity and combination in the national interest. In the words of one of our leaders, India is 'learning through her own struggles all her lessons of a free and self-regulated and self-sustained national life.' Those lessons, there is but too much reason to say, are being learnt in spite of, not with the help of, England.

The gift of a seat on the Executive Council, or of a few official posts, more or less, no more fulfils or tends to fulfil the objective of the National movement, than a seat in the cabinet for an Ulster Unionist would meet the Irish demand for Home Rule, or the elevation of Mr. Burns to the Presidency of the Board of Trade, the socialist demand for the nationalisation of natural monopolies. The objective of the true nationalist is control of government—not a share in the administration of his country.

None can be truly qualified to educate or govern, who cannot, in the words of the great Sinhalese chronicle, 'make themselves one with the religion and the people.' "When" says Confucius "the prince loves what the people love and hates what the people hate, then is he what is called the father of the people." These ideals are absolutely unattainable by Englishmen in India. However conscientious a Civil Servant or a Governor may be, his heart is far away in England, and he counts the days till he returns. He is, at best, the conscientious bailiff of an absentee landlord; a person profoundly ignorant of the nature of the soil that he attempts to cultivate.

It is not out of hatred for England that India demands her freedom, it is partly for England's sake. The ownership of India is a chain about England's neck,—a weight not less hurtful because scarcely felt as such. "When we learn to sing that Britons never will be masters we shall make an end of slavery," are true words spoken by a well-known English writer. No nation can serve faithfully two ideals without hypocrisy. In Italy, in Japan, in Persia, in Turkey, England's sympathies have been or still are with the great idealistic movements; only in Egypt and India, where these movements clash with her material interests, her attitude is different! The exercise of despotic power in India provides for England a large and powerful reactionary element in her own governance. Those who on the plea of necessity resort in India to punishment without trial, or the suppression of free speech, will be ready on the same plea to fall back upon the same resources in the government of Ireland or the suppression of the unemployed, or of women, in England. England may lose something of her own liberties, through the denial of liberty to others. Harmful too to England is that change that comes over nearly all Englishmen (of course, with noble exceptions), in the course of weeks or months after they set foot in India as rulers; the attitude of patronage and contempt, the conceit and aloofness of the Anglo-Indian do not drop like a mantle from his shoulder when he retires to England to spend the rest of his days in the enjoyment of an Indian pension, and qualities thus fostered scarcely tend to the progress of England towards an ideal life. More obviously and directly injurious to England's moral fibre are the partial justice she administers, and her reliance —an unavoidable reliance it may be for one in her position—upon informers, underpaid police and spies. As she sows, she must also reap; and it cannot be that she should escape the reaction upon herself of stooping to such means. For England's truest interests it were far best that she should be free of such a burden. The life of European nations is as yet so little ordered, so chaotic and unorganised that it were well for each of them had they more time to set in order their own house; but Imperialism and social reform are incompatible.

We do not stand alone in the awakening of our national genius; the phenomenon is world-wide, and may be studied in lands so far apart as Ireland and Japan. The movement is a protest of the human spirit against a premature and artificial cosmopolitanism which would destroy in nations, as modern education destroys in individuals, the special genius of each. It would take too long to correlate all the phases of nationalism in East and West; but to illustrate its unity of purpose, and the character of its idealism, I make just two quotations from its current literature elsewhere.

The first is a passage from a pamphlet issued by the Gaelic League, replacing only the word 'Irishmen,' by the word 'Indians.'

"Indians we all are, and therefore our only possible perfection consists in the development of the Indian nature we have inherited from our forefathers. Centuries of real development, of civilisation, of noble fidelity to all the highest ideals men can worship, have fixed for ever the national character of India; and if we be not true to that character, if we be not genuine Indians, we can never be perfect men, full and strong men, able to do a true man's part for God and motherland. Our forefathers are our best models and patterns; they alone can show us what our common Indian nature can and ought to be. We must copy their greatness and their goodness; truly worthy are they of affectionate and reverent imitation, for were they not men of renown in their day, men of highest saintliness, of Indian genius and learning and love of learning, of might and valour or the dread field of battle—saints, scholars, heroes ?.... Look to your forefathers, read of them, speak of them; not in unworthy mendicant eloquence, nor yet in vulgar boasting about our ancient glories while we squat down in disgraceful content with our present degeneracy, nor least of all in miserable petty controversy with the hireling liars who calumniate our dear India. No! but to learn from them what you ought to be, what God destined Indians to be."

One of the most beautiful of exhortations to a people in a position akin to ours, is the message which Pierre Loti addresses to the young Egyptians:

"Reawaken," he says, "before it be too late. Defend yourselves against this disintegrating invasion—not indeed by violence,* not by inhospitableness or bad temper—but by despising this Western crowd that overwhelms you when it is weary of us. Try to preserve not only your traditions and your beautiful Arab tongue, but also all that went to make the grace and mystery of your town, the refined luxury of your homes. This is not a question of the fancies of artists, it is your national dignity that is in danger. You were *Orientals* (I speak with respect when I use this word, that implies a past of early civilisation, and of pure greatness), but, a few years more, and if you do not take heed, they will have made mere Levantine courtiers of you, interested only in the enhancement of land-values and speculations in cotton."

It is in this spirit that the other nations look to us for sincerity in our lives; shall we answer them with lies or truth? Upon that answer depends our future as a nation.

The inspiration of our Nationalism must be not hatred or self-seeking; but Love, first of India, and secondly of England and of the World. The highest ideal of nationality is service; and it is because this service is impossible for us so long as we are politically and spiritually dominated by any Western civilisation, that we are bound to achieve our freedom. It is in this spirit that we must say to Englishmen, that we will achieve this

* Nothing could be more futile than a reliance upon violence as a means of achieving Indian national independence. It is not by destruction, but only through self-development that that end can be achieved.

freedom, if they will, with their consent and with their help; but if they will not, then without their consent and in spite of their resistance.

ANANDA K. COOMARASWAMY.

Campden, December 1909.

P.S. *I am indebted to Mr. Vincent A. Smith for the photograph reproduced on Plate IV., to Mr. E. B. Havell for Plate V, and to Major S. C. Basu for Plate VI.*

CHAPTER I.

The Deeper Meaning of the Struggle.

THE world is now familiar with the phenomenon commonly known as the "Unrest in India." In this unrest or struggle, there have been many more or less dramatic episodes, that have called attention to its existence, otherwise often ignored, sometimes unsuspected. We have had, for example, the series of events connected with the partition of Bengal, the deportation and imprisonment of many Indian leaders without trial, the resignation of a Lieutenant-Governor, attempted assassinations, the use of bombs, innumerable press prosecutions, the suppression of free speech, and on the other hand, some attempts at political reform. These things are signs; but of what struggle, what desire?

So much depends upon our conception of the issues at stake. India for the Indians! True; but why? Is it that we may have, or that we may be, and give? Do we fight with attachment to the fruits of works, such as political rights and commercial prosperity; or do we fight for an idea, the duty of self-realisation for the sake of others? If it is for an idea that we fight, victory is assured, if only for a material end, it may be that there also we shall win—or it may be not—but if we do win, it is not obvious what the great gain to humanity will be. Five hundred years hence it will matter little to humanity whether a few Indians, more or less, have held official posts in India, or a few million bales of cloth been manufactured in Bombay or Lancashire factories; but it will matter much whether the great ideals of Indian culture have been carried forward or allowed to die. It is with these that Indian Nationalism is essentially concerned, and upon these that the fate of India as a nation depends.

Our struggle is part of a wider one, the conflict between the ideals of Imperialism and the ideals of Nationalism. Between these two ideals the world has now to choose. Upon that choice depends the salvation of much that is absolutely essential to the future greatness of civilisation and the richness of the world's culture. For Imperialism involves the subordination of many nationalities to one; a subordination not merely political and economic, but also moral and intellectual. Nationalism is inseparable from the idea of Internationalism, recognising the rights and worth of other nations to be even as one's own. For Britain we cannot speak; but for ourselves, the ideal is that of Nationalism and Internationalism. We feel that loyalty for us consists in loyalty to the idea of an Indian nation, politically, economically and intellectually free; that is, we believe in India for the Indians; but if we do so, it is not merely because we want our own India for ourselves, but because we believe that every nation has its own part to play in the long tale of human progress, and that nations, which are not free to develop their own individuality and own character, are also unable to make the contribution to the sum of human culture which the world has a right to expect of them.

The world may be likened to a vast, as yet unordered garden, having diverse soils and aspects, some watered, some arid, some plain, some mountain; the different parts of which should properly be tended by different gardeners, having experience of diverse qualities of soil and aspect; but certain ones have seized upon the plots of others, and attempted to replace the plants natural to those plots, with others more acceptable or profitable to themselves. We have not to consider only the displaced gardeners, who naturally do not admire and are not grateful for the changes introduced into their plots; but to ask whether these proceedings are beneficial to the owner of the garden, for whom the gardeners work. Who is this owner but the Folk of the World of the future, which is ever becoming the present? Shall they be glad or sorry if uniformity has replaced diversity, if but one type of vegetation is to be found within their garden, flourishing perhaps in one part, but sickly in another; what of the flowers that might have flourished in that other part had they not been swept away?

The world has progressed from the idea of individual slavery to that of individual freedom; it has become an instinct to believe that men are equal at least to this degree, that every man must be regarded as an end in himself; but progress is only now being made from the idea of national slavery (Empire) to that of national freedom (Internationalism). The dominant nations have to learn that nations no less than men are ends in themselves. They have yet to realise that a nation can no more ultimately justify the ownership of other nations, than a man can justify the ownership of other men; and that it is not by the withdrawal of responsibility that character is strengthened.

Many of the difficulties that beset the path of Indian nationality are real. The one thing strange to us is the delight with which they are insisted on, as though the possibility of an Indian nation, conscious of its past, and led by hope of days to come, were in itself an evil thing. Why is there not rejoicing at a nation's birth, or adolescence? For to all men the gift is given, and to all is brought the fame. "How many things shalt thou quicken, how many shalt thou slay! How many things shalt thou

B 2

waken, how many gather to sleep! How many things shalt thou scatter, how many gather and keep! O me, how thy love shall cherish, how thine hate shall wither and burn! How the hope shall be sped from thy right hand, nor the fear to thy left return! O thy deeds that men shall sing of!.... O Victory yet to be!"

Let us not forget that in setting this ideal of Nationalism before us, we are not merely striving for a right, but accepting a duty that is binding on us, that of self-realisation to the utmost for the sake of others. India's ancient contribution to the civilisation of the world does not and never can justify her children in believing that her work is done. There is work yet for her to do, which, if not done by her, will remain for ever undone. We may not shirk our part in the re-organisation of life, which is needed to make life tolerable under changed conditions. It is for us to show that industrial production can be organised on socialistic lines without converting the whole world into groups of state-owned factories. It is for us to show that great and lovely cities can be built again, and things of beauty made in them, without the pollution of the air by smoke or the poisoning of the river by chemicals; for us to show that man can be the master, not the slave of the mechanism he himself has created.

It is for us to proclaim that wisdom is greater than knowledge; for us to make clear anew that art is something more than manual dexterity, or the mere imitation of natural forms. It is for us to investigate the physical and supersensual faculties anew in the light of the discoveries of Physical Science and to show that Science and Faith may be reconciled on a higher plane than any reached as yet. It is for us to intellectualise and spiritualise the religious conceptions of the West, and to show that the true meaning of religious tolerance is not the refraining from persecution, but the real belief that different religions need not be mutually exclusive, the conviction that they are all good roads, suited to the varying capacities of those that tread them, and leading to one end.

This and much more is our allotted task. Other peoples have found other work to do, some of which we may well share, and some leave to those still best fitted to perform it; but let us not turn from our own task to attempt the seemingly more brilliant or more useful work of others. "Better is one's own duty, though insignificant, than even the well-executed duty of another." Let us not be tempted by all the kingdoms of the earth; granted there is much that we have not, which others have, and which we may acquire from them; what is the price to be? "What shall it profit a man if he gain the whole world and lose his own soul?"

Think of our duty from another point of view; is not the ancient virtue of hospitality binding on us? Yet now the shame of hospitality refused is ours; how many have come to India, reverencing her past, ready to learn of her still, and have been sent empty away! The student of Social Economy finds a highly organised society in the process of disintegration without any of the serious and constructive effort required for its re-organisation under changed conditions; the student of Architecture finds a tradition living still, but scorned by a people devoted to the imitation of their rulers, building copies of English palaces and French villas in the very presence of men who still know how to build, and under the shadow of buildings as noble as any that the world has seen. The student of Fine Art is shown inferior imitations of the latest European 'styles,' where he should find some new and living revelation; the decorative artist sees the traditional craftsmen of India thrown out of employment by the mechanical vulgarities of Birmingham and

Manchester, without the least effort made to preserve for future generations the accumulated skill and cunning of centuries of the manufacture of materials and wares which have commanded the admiration of the world. The musician of other lands hears little but the gramophone or the harmonium in India; the man of religion finds the crudest materialism replacing a reasoned metaphysic; the lover of freedom beholds a people who can be imprisoned or deported for indefinite periods without trial, and too divided amongst themselves to offer adequate resistance to this *lawlessness;* in a word, every man seeking to widen his own outlook, sees but his own face distorted in an Indian mirror.

It is from this inhospitableness, this cowardice, that the call of the Motherland must waken us. We are conscious that the best in us is sleeping still; but when the sleeper wakes, who knoweth what shall come of it? One thing at least we are certain of, that the awakening must be no waking in a prison cell, but that of a free man, "full of good hopes, of steady purpose, perfect strength."* It is for this that we are stirred, for this that we shall suffer; and this is the deeper meaning of the great Indian struggle for freedom.

* Taittiriya Upanishad.

CHAPTER II.

Indian Nationality.

WHAT are the things which make possible national self-consciousness, which constitute nationality? Certainly a unity of some sort is essential. There are certain kinds of unity, however, which are not essential, and others which are insufficient. Racial unity, for example, does not constitute the Negroes of North America a nation. Racial unity is not even an essential; the British nation is perhaps more composed of diverse racial elements than any other, but it has none the less a strong national consciousness. To take another example, many of the most Irish of the Irish are of English origin; Keating and Emmet, for instance, were of Norman descent; but neither they nor their labours were on that account less a part or an expression of Irish national feeling and self-consciousness. Neither is a common and distinctive language an essential; Switzerland is divided among three languages, and Ireland between two.

Two essentials of nationality there are,—a geographical unity, and a common historic evolution or culture. These two India possesses superabundantly, beside many lesser unities which strengthen the historical tradition.

The fact of India's geographical unity is apparent on the map, and is never, I think, disputed. The recognition of social unity is at least as evident to the student of Indian culture. The idea has been grasped more than once by individual rulers,—Asoka,

Vikramāditya and Akbar. It was recognized before the Mahābhārata was written; when Yudhishtira performed the Rājasuya sacrifice on the occasion of his inauguration as sovereign, a great assembly (*sabhā*—simply the *gam-sabhāva*, or village council on a larger scale) was held, and to this assembly came Bhīma, Dhritarashtra and his hundred sons, Ṣubala (King of Gandhāra), etc.... and others from the extreme south and north (Dravida, Ceylon and Kashmīr). In legends, too, we meet with references to councils or motes of the gods, held in the Himālayas, whither they repaired to further common ends. No one can say that any such idea as that of a Federated States of India is altogether foreign to the Indian mind. But more than all this, there is evidence enough that the founders of Indian culture and civilization and religion (whether you call them rishis or men) had this unity in view; and the manner in which this idea pervades the whole of Indian culture is the explanation of the possibility of its rapid realisation now. Is it for nothing that India's sacred shrines are many and far apart; that one who would visit more than one or two of these must pass over hundreds of miles of Indian soil? Benares is the sacred city of Buddhist and Hindu alike; Samanala in Ceylon is a holy place for Buddhist, Hindu and Muhammadan. Is there no meaning in the sacred reverence for the Himālayas which every Indian feels? Is the *geis* altogether meaningless which forbids the orthodox Hindu to leave the Motherland and cross the seas? Is the passionate adoration of the Indian people for the Ganges thrown away? How much is involved in such phrases as 'The Seven Great Rivers' (of India)! The Hindu in the north repeats the mantram:

> Om gangē cha yamune chaiva godāvarī, sarasvatī,
> narmade, sindhu kaverī jale' smin sannidhim kuru.*

*** "Hail! O ye Ganges, Jamna, Godavari, Sarasvati, Narmada, Sindhu and Kaveri, come and approach these waters."**

when performing ceremonial ablutions; the Buddhist in Ceylon uses the same prayer on a similar occasion. Or take the epics, the foundation of Indian education and culture; or a poem like the Megha Duta, the best known and most read work of Kalidasa. Are not these expressive of love for and knowledge of the Motherland? The 'holy land' of the Indian is not a far-off Palestine but the Indian land itself.

The whole of Indian culture is so pervaded with this idea of India as THE LAND, that it has never been necessary to insist upon it overmuch, for no one could have supposed it otherwise. "Every province within the vast boundaries fulfils some necessary part in the completion of a nationality. No one place repeats the specialised functions of another." Take, for example, Ceylon (whose people are now the most denationalised of any in India); can we think of India as complete without Ceylon? Ceylon is unique as the home of Pāli literature and Southern Buddhism, and in its possession of a continuous chronicle invaluable as a check upon some of the more uncertain data of Indian Chronology. Sinhalese art, Sinhalese religion, and the structure of Sinhalese society, bring most vividly before us certain aspects of early Hindu culture, which it would be hard to find so perfectly reflected in any other part of modern India. The noblest of Indian epics, the love-story of Rāma and Sītā, unites Ceylon and India in the mind of every Indian, nor is this more so in the south than in the north. In later times, the histories of northern India and Ceylon were linked in Vijaya's emigration, then by Asoka's missions (contemporaneous with earliest ripples of the wave of Hindu influence which passed beyond the Himālayas to impress its ideals on the Mongolian east); and later still a Sinhalese princess became a Rājput bride, to earn the perpetual love of her adopted people by her fiery death, the death which every Rājput woman would have preferred above dishonour. To this day her name is remembered by the peoples of northern India, as that of one who was the flower and crown of beauty and heroism. And just in such wise are all the different parts of India bound together by a common historical tradition and ties of spiritual kinship; none can be spared, nor can any live independent of the others.

The diverse peoples of India are like the parts of some magic puzzle, seemingly impossible to fit together, but falling easily into place when once the key is known; and the key is that realization of the fact that the parts do fit together, which we call national self-consciousness. I am often reminded of the Cairene girl's lute, in the tale of Miriam and Ali Nur-al-Din. It was kept in a "green satin bag with slings of gold." She took the bag, "and opening it, shook it, whereupon there fell thereout two-and-thirty pieces of wood, which she fitted one into other, male into female, and female into male, till they became a polished lute of Indian workmanship. Then she uncovered her wrists and laying the lute in her lap, bent over it with the bending of mother over babe, and swept the strings with her finger-tips; whereupon it moaned and resounded and after its olden home yearned; and it remembered the waters that gave it drink and the earth whence it sprang and wherein it grew and it minded the carpenters who cut it and the polishers who polished it and the merchants who made it their merchandise and the ships that shipped it; and it cried and called aloud and moaned and groaned; and it was as if she asked it of all these things and it answered her with the tongue of the case." Just such an instrument is India, composed of many parts seemingly irreconcileable, but in reality each one cunningly designed towards a common end; so, too, when these parts are set together and attuned, will India tell of the earth from which she sprang, the waters that gave her drink, and the Shapers that have shaped her being; nor will she be then the idle singer of an empty day, but the giver of hope to all, when hope will most avail, and most be needed.

I have spoken so far only of Hindus and Hindu culture; and if so it is because Hindus form the main part of the population of India, and Hindu culture the main part of Indian culture: but the quotation just made from Arabian literature leads on to the consideration of the great part which Muhammadans, and Persi-Arabian culture have played in the historic evolution of India, as we know it to-day. It would hardly be possible to think of an India in which no Great Mughal had ruled, no Tāj been built, or to which Persian art and literature were wholly foreign. Few great Indian rulers have displayed the genius for statesmanship which Akbar had, a greater religious toleration than he. On the very morrow of conquest he was able to dispose of what is now called the Hindu-Muhammadan difficulty very much more successfully than it is now met in Bengal; for he knew that there could be no real diversity of interest between Hindu and Muhammedan, and treated them with an impartiality which we suspect to be greater than that experienced in Bengal to-day. It was not his interest to divide and rule. Like most Eastern rulers (who can never be foreigners in the same way that a Western ruler necessarily must be) he identified himself with his kingdom, and had no interests that clashed with its interests. This has, until modern times, been always a characteristic of an invader's or usurper's rule in India, that the ruler has not attempted to remain in his own distant country and rule the conquered country from afar, farming it like an absentee landlord, but has identified himself with it. The beneficent rule of Elāla, a Tamil usurper in Ceylon two centuries before Christ, was so notorious that deep respect was paid to the site of his tomb more than 2,000 years later; and to mention a more modern case, the 18th century Tamil (Hindu) ruler, Kīrti Srī and his two brothers, so identified themselves with the Sinhalese (Buddhist) people as to have deserved the chronicler's remark that they were "one with the religion and the people." To show that such a situation is still possible, it will suffice to cite the States of Hyderabad, Baroda and Gwalior.

Even suppose the differences that separate the Indian communities to be twice as great as they are said to be, they are nothing compared with the difference between the Indian and the European. Western rule is inevitably alien rule, in a far deeper sense than the rule of Hindus by Muhammadans or the reverse could be. And what does alien rule mean? "The government of a people by itself," says John Stuart Mill, "has a meaning and a reality, but such a thing as the government of one people by another does not and cannot exist. One people may keep another as a warren or preserve for its own use, a place to make money in, a human farm to be worked for the profit of its own inhabitants." No cant of the "white man's burden" alters the stern logic of these facts; to us it appears that the domination of the East by the West is a menace to the evolution of the noblest ideal of humanity; the "white man's burden" translated into the language of Asiatic thought becomes "the white peril;" and this is not because we despise the achievements of Western civilisation, or fail to appreciate the merits of Europeans as such, but because we think that a whole world of Europeans would be a poor place, quite as poor as a whole world of Indians or Chinamen. We feel it then our duty to realise our unity and national self-consciousness in concrete form, as much for the advantage of others as of ourselves; and this without any feeling of bitterness or exclusiveness towards other races, though perhaps for a time such feelings may be inevitable. And to show what spirit moves us we have such a statement of belief in the unity of the Indian people, as the credo of Shiv Narayen; and the beautiful national song, called 'Bande Mātaram' ('Hail! Motherland') which expresses the aims and the power of the awakened Indian nation, as the Marseillaise embodied the ideal of awakened France, or as those of Ireland are expressed in the songs of Ethna Carberry.

Their words are not the hysterical utterance of a people uncertain of their unity or doubtful of their future. They express the Indian recognition of the Motherland, their quiet but profound assurance of her greatness and beauty, and their consciousness of the high calling which is hers. They voice the hope of an INDIAN NATION, which shall not be disappointed.

CHAPTER III.

Mata Bharata.

THERE was once a tall, fair woman,—not indeed young, no one could have thought that—but serene to the uttermost and possessed of great patience and grace. In years past she had been famed for wisdom, and the wise men of the world had sat at her feet and carried away her teachings to the ends of the earth. But now she was older, and a little weary, and the light in her eyes served only as a star for the few who still beheld reality behind appearance. She was, moreover, wealthy, and many had sought her hand, and of these, one whom she loved least had possessed her body for many years; and now there came another and stranger wooer with promises of freedom and peace, and protection for her children; and she believed in him, and laid her hand in his.

For a time it was well, her new lord was contented with the wealth of her treasure houses and gave her the peace of neglect. But ere long he took more interest in his cold bride and her children, and said to himself, "This woman has strange ways unlike my own and those of my people, and her thoughts are not my thoughts; but she shall be trained and educated, that she may know what I know, and that the world may say that I have moulded her mind into the paths of progress." For he knew not of her ancient wisdom, and she seemed to him slow of mind, and lacking in that practical ability on which he prided himself.

And while these thoughts were passing in his mind, some of her children were roused against him, by reason of his robbing them of power and interfering with the rights and laws that regulated their relations to each other; for they feared that their ancient heritage would pass away for ever. But still the mother dreamed of peace and rest and would not hear the children's cry, but helped to subdue their waywardness; and ere long all was quiet again. But the wayward children loved not their new father and could not understand their mother. And their new father turned to other ways, and sent the children to schools where they were taught his language and his thoughts, and how great his people were, and self-sacrificing; and from what unrest and wretchedness he had saved their mother, and with no thought of gain or profit; and they were taught, too, to forget their ancient glory and from the height of the new learning to despise their ancient manners.

But now another thing happened; the mother bore a child to the foreign lord, and he was pleased thereat, and deemed that she (for it was a girl) should be a woman after his own heart, even as the daughters of his own people, and she should be fair and wealthy, and a bride for a son of his people. But when this child was born, the mother was roused from her dream, and lived only for the girl, and she grew up to remind the mother of her own youth, and favoured the foreign lord little; yet she had somewhat of his energy and turn for practical affairs. The mother talked long and deeply with her, and the foreign lord did not take it aught amiss, for he deemed that all must go even as he, such a great man, would have it go. And he got teachers, and she was taught the wisdom and manners of his people. But in secret the mother taught her the ancient wisdom, and her heart was turned away from her father and his people and his teaching. And the mother was content; and now she was white-haired and weak with age, and a time came when she passed hence, for her work was done. And the foreign lord himself grew a little weary, for there were troubles in his own land, and some had said that he was a tyrant in a foreign land; and thereby his heart was pained, for had not he spent his life for others, and surely the labourer was worthy of his hire? But the girl grew strong, and would brook little of her father's tyranny, and she was a mother to the children of the children who came before her, and she was called the Mother by all; and perhaps she and her mother were after all the same. One day there arose murmurings amongst the children as of old, and they said that they needed no foreign lord to take their revenues and school their minds. Still they were subdued with a high hand and some were cast in prison, or worse, for the father was a patriarch of the old type and deemed it amiss that he had not the power of life and death over all his subject people. But now they would not brook his tyranny—for he himself unwittingly had taught them that the king-days were over, and made them dream of freedom.

All these trials were upon him, and he grew old and weary; and the young mother (she would be mother of all she said, but wedded unto none) helped all the children and taught them to love and help each other and to call her mother; and she left the foreign lord and went to live in a place apart, where the children came to her for counsel. And when the foreign lord would have stopped it, she was not there, but elsewhere; and it seemed that she was neither here nor there, but everywhere.

*　*　*　*　*　*

And this tale is yet unfinished; but the ending is not far away, and may be foreseen.

PLATE 1.

NATARĀJA.

CHAPTER IV.

The Aims and Methods of Indian Art.

THE extant remains of Indian art cover a period of more than two thousand years. During this time many schools of thought have flourished and decayed, invaders of many races have poured into India and contributed to the infinite variety of her intellectual resources; countless dynasties have ruled and passed away; and so we do not wonder that many varieties of artistic expression remain to record for us, in a language of their own, something of the ideas and the ideals of many peoples, their hopes and fears, their faith and their desire. But just as through all Indian schools of thought there runs like a golden thread the fundamental idealism of the Upanishads, the Vedānta, so in all Indian art there is a unity that underlies all its bewildering variety. This unifying principle is here also Idealism, and this must of necessity have been so, for the synthesis of Indian thought is one, not many.

What, after all, is the secret of Indian greatness? Not a dogma or a book; but the great open secret that all knowledge and all truth are absolute and infinite, waiting not to be created, but to be found; the secret of the infinite superiority of intuition, the method of direct perception, over the intellect, regarded as a mere organ of discrimination. There is about us a storehouse of the As-Yet-Unknown, infinite and inexhaustible; but to this wisdom, the way of access is not through intellectual activity. The intuition that reaches to

C

it, we call Imagination and Genius. It came to Sir Isaac Newton when he saw the apple fall, and there flashed across his brain the Law of Gravity. It came to the Buddha as he sat through the silent night in meditation, and hour by hour all things became apparent to him; he knew the exact circumstances of all beings that have ever been in the endless and infinite worlds; at the twentieth hour he received the divine insight by which he saw all things within the space of the infinite sakvalas as clearly as if they were close at hand; then came still deeper insight, and he perceived the cause of sorrow and the path of knowledge, 'He reached at last the exhaustless source of truth.' The same is true of all 'revelation'; the Veda (*sruti*), the eternal *Logos*, 'breathed forth by Brahma,' in whom it survives the destruction and creation of the Universe, is 'seen,' or 'heard,' not made, by its human authors. . . . The reality of such perception is witnessed to by every man within himself upon rare occasions and on an infinitely smaller scale. It is the inspiration of the poet. It is at once the vision of the artist, and the imagination of the natural philosopher.

There is a close analogy between the aims of art and of science. Descriptive science is, of course, concerned only with the record of appearances; but art and theoretical science have much in common. The imagination is required for both; both illustrate that natural tendency to seek the one in the many, to formulate natural laws, which is expressed in the saying that the human mind functions naturally towards unity. The aim of the trained scientific or artistic imagination is to conceive (*concipio*, lay hold of) invent (*invenio*, to light upon) or imagine (visualise) some unifying truth previously unsuspected or forgotten. The theory of evolution or of electrons or atoms; the rapid discovery (unveiling) by a mathematical genius of the answer to an abstruse calculation; the conception that flashes into the artist's mind, all these represent some true vision of the Idea underlying phenomenal experience, some message from the 'exhaustless source of truth.' Ideal art is thus rather a spiritual discovery, than a creation. It differs from science in its concern primarily with subjective things, things as they are for us, rather than in themselves. Empirical science is a record of 'facts'; art is the controlled and rhythmic expression of emotion. But both art and science have the common aim of unity; of formulating natural laws.

The real aim, both of art and of science, is to reach the type, the Platonic Idea. Art seeks this end deductively and synthetically, empirical science only inductively, and analytically.

Genius may be metaphorically described as a thinning of the veil, or a permeability of the diaphragm, which, as it were, separates the conscious from the superconscious self. It is characteristic of genius that ideas, inspiration, appear to arrive altogether from outside the ordinary (*jagrat*) consciousness. They originate in fact in a region external to the mere intellect (*manas*), being apprehended by the reason (*buḍḍhi*) acting as a sixth sense organ (intuition). As unity is the characteristic of buddhic consciousness, so it is characteristic of ideas thus apprehended, that they are 'seen' or 'heard' as a whole, and have as it were to be subsequently disentangled in space and time.

A great poem or picture or musical composition is thus first apprehended as a unity; by concentration, the details of this presentation may be developed, like the image on a photographic plate. The most effective genius is one in whom this process of development is most perfectly accomplished, who sees and hears, and is able to retain the presentation most completely.

C 2

The artist has, indeed, a sense almost of terror lest the vision should be lost before he is able to impress it upon his empirical consciousness. It is owing to the same cause that we feel the sense of irreparable loss which is associated with the destruction of a work of real art; for by such destruction something has been taken out of the circle of our ordinary consciousness, which perhaps can never be restored to it.

It is said of a certain famous craftsman that, when designing, he seemed not to be making, but merely to be outlining a pattern that he already saw upon the paper before him. The true artist does not 'compose' (put-together) his picture, but 'sees' it; his desire is to represent his vision in the material terms of line and colour. To the great painter such pictures come continually, often too rapidly and too confusedly to be caught and disentangled. Could he but control his mental vision, define and hold it! It is here that the relation between the methods of the Indian worshipper and the Indian artist becomes significant.

"Fickle is the mind, froward, forceful, and stiff; I deem it as hard to check as is the wind." Yet by "constant labour and passionlessness it may be held," and this concentration of mental vision has been from long ago the very method of Indian religion, and the control of thought its ideal of worship. It is thus that the Hindu worships daily his Ishta Devatā, the special aspect of divinity that is to him all and more than the Patron Saint is to the Catholic. Simple men may worship such an one as Ganesa, 'easy to reach, not far away; some can make the greater effort needed to reach even Natarāja; and only for those whose heart is set upon the Unconditioned, is a mental image useless as a centre of thought. These last are few; and for those that adore an Ishta Devatā, or conditioned and special aspect of God, worship of Him consists first in the recitation of the brief mnemonic *mantram* detailing His attributes, and then in silent concentration of thought upon the corresponding mental image. These mental images are of the same nature as those the artist sees, and the process of visualisation is the same.

Here, for example, is a verse from one of the imager's technical books (the *Rūpāvaliya*):

"These are the marks of Siva, a glorious visage, three eyes, a bow and an arrow, a serpent garland, ear-flowers, a rosary, four hands, a *trisūla*, a noose, a deer, hands betokening mildness and beneficence, a garment of tiger skin, His *vāhan* a bull of the hue of the chank."*

It may be compared with the Dhyāna mantrams used in the daily meditation of a Hindu upon the Gāyatrī visualised as a Goddess:

"In the evening Sarasvatī should be meditated upon as the essence of the Sāma Veda, fair of face, having two arms, holding a *trisūla* and a drum, old, and as Rudrānī, the bull her *vāhan*."

Almost the whole philosophy of Indian art is contained in the verse of Sukrācārya's *Sukranītisāra* which enjoins this method of visualisation upon the imager:

"Let the builder establish images in temples by meditation on the deities who are the objects of his devotion; for the successful achievement of (this) *dhyāna yoga* (yoga of contemplation) the elements and characteristics of the image are described in books to be dwelt upon in detail. In no other way, not even by direct and immediate vision of an actual object, is it possible to be so absorbed in contemplation, as thus in the making of images."

It cannot be too clearly understood that the mere representation of nature is never the aim of

* *i.e.*, riding upon a snow-white bull.

Indian art. Probably no truly Indian sculpture has been wrought direct from a living model, or any religious painting copied from the life. Possibly no Hindu artist of the old schools ever drew from nature at all. His store of memory pictures, his power of visualisation and his imagination were for his purpose finer means; for he desired to suggest the Idea behind sensuous appearance, not to give the detail of the seeming reality, that was in truth but *māyā*, illusion. For in spite of the pantheistic accommodation of infinite truth to the capacity of finite minds, whereby God is conceived as entering into all things, Nature remains to the Hindu a veil, not a revelation; and art is to be something more than a mere imitation of this *māyā*, it is to manifest what lies behind. To mistake the *māyā* for reality were error indeed:

"Men of no understanding think of Me, the unmanifest as having manifestation, knowing not My higher being to be changeless, supreme.

"Veiled by the Magic of My Rule (*Yoga-Māyā*), I am not revealed to all the world; this world is bewildered, and perceives Me not as birthless and unchanging" (*Bhagavad Gītā*, *VII.*, 24, 25).

Of course, an exception to these principles in Indian art may be pointed to in the Indo-Persian school of portrait miniature; and this work does show that it was no lack of power that in most other cases kept the Indian artist from realistic representation. But here the deliberate aim is portraiture, not the representation of Divinity or Superman. And even in the portraits there are many ideal qualities apparent. In purely Hindu and religious art, however, even portraits are felt to be lesser art than the purely ideal and abstract representations; and such realism as we find, for example, in the Ajantā paintings, is due to the keenness of the artist's memory of familiar things, not to absorption in the imitation of appearances.

For realism that thus represents keenness of memory picture, strength of imagination, there is room in all art; duly restrained, it is so much added power. But realism which is of the nature of imitation of an object actually seen at the time of painting is quite antipathetic to imagination, and finds no place in the ideal of Indian art.

Much of the criticism applied to works of art in modern times is based upon the idea of 'truth to nature.' The first thing for which many people look in a work of art, is for something to recognize; and if the representation is of something they have not seen, or symbolizes some unfamiliar abstract idea, it is, for them, thereby self-condemned as untrue to nature.

What, after all, is reality and what is truth? The Indian thinker answers that nature, the phenomenal world that is, is known to him only through sensation, and that he has no warrant for supposing that sensations convey to him any adequate conception of the intrinsic reality of things in themselves; nay, he denies that they have any such reality apart from himself. At most, natural forms are but incarnations of ideas, and each is but an incomplete expression.

It has never been supposed by Oriental artists that the object of art is the reproduction of the external forms of nature. Such a conception, in modern Europe, is the natural product of a life divorced from beauty. Pictorial imitations of nature are the substitute in which men seek for compensation for the unloveliness of an artificial life. We are nowhere able to observe that realistic art is or has anywhere been the ideal of men whose lives have been lived—as in Egypt, India, Persia or Mediæval Europe—in the real intimacy of nature herself. The imitation of nature, indeed, has been seen by all true artists and philosophers to be both impossible and unnecessary. "For why," as

Deussen says "should the artist wish to imitate laboriously and inadequately what nature offers everywhere in unattainable profusion?" viz., individual, and in so far, limited, manifestations of Ideas?

In the realm of nature we see the thousandfold repeated reflections of Ideas, in these individual manifestations. It is for the artist, by *yoga*, that is, by self-identification with the soul of such reflections, fully to understand them and explain their inner significance. "Guided by an insight into the nature of things which fathoms deeper than all abstract knowledge, he is able to understand the 'half uttered words of nature,' to infer from what she forms that which she intends to form, to anticipate from the direction she takes the end she is unable to reach." But it is further possible, by imagination, the first and essential quality of genius, to apprehend Ideas which, though subsisting in the cosmic consciousness, have not yet assumed, and may never assume, a physically visible form. Such are the forms of gods or nature spirits, and flowers or animals or scenes in 'other worlds'; personifications of abstract qualities and natural forces, and by no means least, the imagined forms of legendary heroes, in which the race-idea finds its most complete expression. This race expression is most perfect when, as is so often the case, hero and god are one.

It is for the artist to portray the ideal world of true reality, the world of imagination, and not the phenomenal world perceived by the senses.

How strangely this art philosophy contrasts with that characteristic of the modern West, so clearly set forth in Browning's poem:

> "But why not do as well as say,....paint these
> Just as they are, careless what comes of it?
> God's works—paint any one....
> ....Have you noticed, now,

Yon cullion's hanging face? A bit of chalk,
And trust me but you should though! How much more
If I drew higher things with the same truth!
That were to take the Prior's pulpit-place,
Interpret God to all of you!"

For such realists, this last is not the function of art; but to us it seems that the very essential function of art is to 'interpret God to all of you!'

Burne-Jones almost alone amongst artists of the modern West seems to have understood art as we in India understand it. To a critic who named as a drawback in the work of a certain artist, that his pictures looked as if he had done them only out of his head, Burne-Jones replied, "The place where I think pictures ought to come from."

Of impressionism as understood in the West, and the claim that breadth is gained by lack of finish, Burne-Jones spoke as an Eastern artist might have done. Breadth could be got "by beautiful finish and bright, clear colour well-matched, rather than by muzzy. They (the Impressionists) do make atmosphere, but they don't make anything else: they don't make beauty, they don't make design, they don't make idea, they don't make anything but atmosphere—and I don't think that's enough—I don't think it's very much." Of realism he spoke thus: "Realism? Direct transcript from Nature? I suppose by the time the 'photographic artist' can give us all the colours as correctly as the shapes, people will begin to find out that the realism they talk about isn't art at all, but science; interesting, no doubt, as a scientific achievement, but nothing more.. ....Transcripts from Nature, what do I want with transcripts? I prefer her own signature; I don't want forgeries more or less skilful........It is the message, the 'burden' of a picture that makes its real value."

At another time he said, "You see, it is these things of the soul that are real....the only real things in the universe."

Of the religiousness of the art he said:

"That was an awful thought of Ruskin's, that artists paint God for the world. There's a lump of greasy pigment at the end of Michael Angelo's hog-bristle brush, and by the time it has been laid on the stucco, there is something there that all men with eyes recognize as divine. Think of what it means. It is the power of bringing God into the world—making God manifest."

"The object of art must be either to please or to exalt; I can't see any other reason for it at all. One is a pretty reason, the other a noble one."

Of 'expression' in imaginative pictures he said:

"Of course my faces have no expression in the sense in which people use the word. How should they have any? They are not portraits of people in paroxysms—paroxysms of terror, hatred, benevolence, desire, avarice, veneration and all the 'passions' and 'emotion' that Le Brun and that kind of person find so *magnifique* in Raphael's later work........The only expression allowable in great portraiture is the expression of character and moral quality, not of anything temporary, fleeting, accidental. Apart from portraiture you don't want even so much, or very seldom: in fact you want only types, symbols, suggestions. The moment you give what people call expression, you destroy the typical characters of heads and degrade them into portraits which stand for nothing." *

Common criticisms of Indian art are based on supposed or real limitations of technical attainment in representation, especially of the figure. In part, it may be answered that so little is known in the West of the real achievement of Indian art, that this idea may be allowed to die a natural death in the course of time; and in part, that technical attainment is only a means, not an end. There is

* Quotations from "Memorials of Edward Burne-Jones," by Lady Burne-Jones, 1904.

an order of importance in the things art means to us....is it not something thus, first, What has the artist to say? and second only, Is his drawing scientifically accurate? Bad drawing is certainly not in itself desirable, nor good drawing a misfortune; but, strange as it may seem, it has always happened in the history of art, that by the time perfection of technique has been attained, inspiration has declined. It was so in Greece, and in Europe after the Renaissance. It almost seems as if concentration upon technique hindered the free working of the imagination a little; if so, however much we desire both, do not let us make any mistake as to which is first.

Also, accuracy is not always even desirable. It has been shown by photography that the galloping horse has never been accurately drawn in art; let us hope it never will be. For art has to make use of abstractions and memory pictures, not of photographs; it is a synthesis, not an analysis. And so the whole question of accuracy is relative; and the last word was said by Leonardo da Vinci: "That drawing is best which by its action best expresses the passion that animates the figure." This is the true impressionism of the East, based on the idea that the whole aim of art is the expression of *rasa*, *i.e.*, passion, in the sense of the above quotation.* Beside this true standard of art criticism, questions of archæological or anatomical accuracy sink into relative insignificance.

It will be seen that impressionism, as now understood in the West, is of a quite different character.

Indian art is essentially religious. The conscious aim of Indian art is the intimation of Divinity. But the Infinite and Unconditioned cannot be expressed in finite terms; and art, unable to portray

* See also pp. 36, 37 below.

Divinity unconditioned, and unwilling to be limited by the limitation of humanity, is in India dedicated to the representation of Gods, who to finite man represent comprehensible aspects of an infinite whole.

Sankarācārya prayed thus: "O Lord, pardon my three sins: I have in contemplation clothed in form Thyself that hast no form; I have in praise described Thee who dost transcend all qualities; and in visiting shrines I have ignored Thine omnipresence." So, too, the Tamil poetess Auvvai was once rebuked by a priest for irreverence, in stretching out her limbs towards an image of God: "You say well, Sir," she answered, "yet if you will point out to me a direction where God is not, I will there stretch out my limbs." But such conceptions, though we know them at heart to be true and absolute, involve a denial of all exoteric truth; they are not enough, or rather they are too much, for ordinary men to live by:

"Exceeding great is the toil of these whose mind is attached to the Unshown; for the Unshown Way is painfully won by them that wear the body.

"But as for them who, having cast all works on Me and given themselves over to Me, worship Me in meditation, with whole hearted *yoga*.

"These speedily I lift up from the sea of death and life, O Pārtha, their minds being set on Me" (*Bhagavad Gītā*, *XII*., 5-7).

And so it is, that "any Indian man or woman will worship at the feet of some inspired wayfarer who tells them that there can be no image of God, that the world itself is a limitation, and go straightway, as the natural consequence, to pour water on the head of the Siva-lingam."* Indian religion has accepted art, as it has accepted life in its entirety, with open eyes. India, with all her passion for

* Okakura, 'Ideals of the East,' p. 65.

renunciation, has never suffered from that terrible blight of the imagination which confuses the ideals of the ascetic and of the citizen The citizen is indeed to be restrained; but the very essence of his method is that he should learn restraint or temperance by life, not by the rejection of life. For him, the rejection of life, called Puritanism, would be *in*-temperance.

What then of the true ascetic,* with his ideal of renunciation? It has been thought by many Hindus and Buddhists, as it has by many Christians, that rapid spiritual progress is compatible only with an ascetic life. The goal before us all is salvation from the limitation of individuality, and realisation of unity with Unconditioned Absolute Being. Before such a goal can be attained even the highest intellectual and emotional attachments must be put away; art, like all else in time and space, must be transcended. Great art suggests ideal forms in terms of the appearances of the phenomenal world; but what is art to one that toils upon the Unshown Way, seeking to transcend all limitations of the human intellect, to reach a plane of being unconditioned even by ideal form? For such an one, the most refined and intellectual delights are but flowery meadows where men may linger and delay, while the strait path to utter truth waits vainly for the traveller's feet. This thought explains the belief that absolute emancipation is hardly won by any but human beings yet incarnate; it is harder for the Gods to attain such release, for their pure and exalted bliss and knowledge are attachments even

* True asceticism is a search for a reality beyond conditioned life. "If we are to be excused for rejecting the arts, it must be not because we are contented to be less than men, but because we long to be more than men."—*William Morris.*

All others who reject the arts, are able to do so only because their ideal is one of purely material prosperity; they are willing to be less than men. *"But Industry without art is brutality." (Ruskin.)*

stronger than these of earth. And so we find such an instruction as this:

"Form, sound, taste, smell, touch, these intoxicate beings; cut off the yearning which is inherent in them."—(*Dhammika Sutta*).

The extreme expressions of this thought seem to us more terrible than even the 'coldness of Christian men to external beauty'; we feel this, for instance, in reading the story of the Buddhist monk, Chitta Gutta, who dwelt in a certain cave for sixty years without ever raising his eyes above the ground so far as to observe the beautifully painted roof; nor was he ever aware of the yearly flowering of a great *nā*-tree before his cave, except through seeing the pollen fallen upon the ground. But Indian thought has never dreamed of imposing such ideals upon the citizen, whose *dharma* lies, not in the renunciation of action, but in right action without attachment to its fruits; and for such, who must ever form the great majority of the people, art is both an aid to, and a means of spiritual progress. This same-sightedness explains to us the seeming paradox, that Hinduism and Buddhism, with their ideals of renunciation, have like Mediæval Christianity been at once the inspiration and the stronghold of art.

Symbolism must be briefly spoken of. Most familiar, but often more exclusively of religious than of artistic significance, is the use of concrete attributes and symbols, such as the serpent garland, the *trisūlà*, and the tiger skin of the verses quoted. More subtle is the symbolism of posture of body or position of the hands: the body in activity or in repose, the hands beseeching, granting, destroying, or in some posture of uttermost abstraction. These symbolisms compose an expressive art speech so easily understood by those familiar with it, that the religious end may be attained even where the artistic value of an image may be small. In greater work they serve both to define and to explain; the mysticism of Oriental art is always expressed in definite forms.

India is wont to suggest the eternal and inexpressible infinities in terms of sensuous beauty. The love of man for woman or for nature are one with his love for God. Nothing is common or unclean. All life is a sacrament, no part of it more so than another, and there is no part of it that may not symbolize eternal and infinite things. In this great same-sightedness the opportunity for art is great. But in this religious art it must not be forgotten that life is not to be represented for its own sake, but for the sake of the Divine expressed in and through it. It is laid down:—

"It is always commendable for the artist to draw the images of gods. To make human figures is wrong, or even unholy. Even a misshapen image of God is always better than an image of man, however beautiful" (Sukrācārya). The doctrine here so sternly stated, means, in other words, that imitation and portraiture are lesser aims than the representation of ideal and symbolic forms: the aim of the highest art must always be the intimation of the Divinity behind all form, rather than the imitation of the form itself. One may, for instance, depict the sport of Krishna with the Gopis, but it must be in a spirit of religious idealism, not for the mere sake of the sensuous imagery itself.

By many students, the sex symbolism of some Indian religious art is misconceived: but to those who comprehend the true spirit of Indian thought, this symbolism drawn from the deepest emotional experiences is proof of the power and truth alike of the religion and the art. India draws no distinctions between sacred and profane love. All love is a divine mystery; it is the recognition of Unity. Indeed the whole distinction of sacred and profane is for India meaningless, and so it is that the relation of the soul to God may be conceived in terms of the passionate adoration of a woman for her lover.

Again, the conception of a personal aspect of the Infinite is not in India, any more than in ancient Egypt, limited to that of a male being. The energic power (*sakti*) of a divinity is symbolised in literature and art as a divine woman. I choose, to illustrate this type of symbolism, the strangely lovely Prajñāpāramitā (Plate II) from Java, now in the Rijks Museum at Leiden. This figure of personified "Transcendent Wisdom", is the *sakti* of the Tāntric Buddha, Ādibuddha, who here in Mahāyāna Buddhism occupies the place of Siva.* She is Nature, the concentration of every intellectual and physical power of matter, represented in a state of complete abstraction and personified as Wisdom. By Her union with the acting spirit (Ādibuddha) are produced the Bodhisattvas† and all the phenomenal universe.

There are thus two main motifs in the sex-symbolism of Indian art, that may be represented by feminine conceptions, and even by the actual embrace of the Divine figures: these are the complete surrender of the soul to God‡—and the reaction between two aspects of a personal Divinity, whence is imagined to arise the whole phenomenal universe after submergence in the formless (*pralaya*).

Few aspects of Indian culture are so often, perhaps so wilfully misunderstood as this sex-symbolism in art. Sufficient tribute to the Indian attitude is paid by Sir Monier Williams, when in referring to the presence of many words of erotic

* "Whose fairer half is the Mother who gave birth to all the fourteen worlds and the animate and inanimate kingdoms thereof."—*Kailayamalai.*

† So in Christianity we find a similar sex-symbolism—"conceived of the Holy Ghost", "only-begotten son", and the like.

‡ "For just as one who dallies with a beloved wife has no consciousness of outer or inner, so the spirit also. dallying with the self whose essence is knowledge, has no consciousness of outer or inner."—*Brihadāranyaka Upanishad*. 4. 3. 21.

PLATE II.

PRAJNĀPĀRAMITĀ.

significance in his Sanskrit Dictionary, he says that "in India the relationship between the sexes is regarded as a sacred mystery, and is never held to be suggestive of improper or indecent ideas." As much could hardly be said for Europe.

The explanation of the possibility of such symbolism lies, as I have indicated above, in the acceptance of all life as religious, no part as profane. In such an idealisation of life itself there lies the strength of Hinduism, and in its absence the weakness of modern Christianity. The latter is puritanical; it has no concern with art or agriculture, craft or sex or science. The natural result is that these are secularised, and that men concerned with these vital sides of life must either preserve their life and their religion apart in separate water-tight compartments, or let religion go. The Church cannot well complain of the indifference of men to religion when she herself has cut off from religion, and delimited as 'profane', the physical and mental activities and delights of life itself. Passing through the great galleries of modern art, nothing is more impressive than the fact that none of it is religious. I do not merely mean that there are no Madonnas and no crucifixes; but that there is no evidence of any union of the artistic with the religious sense. The same is true of dancing and music. Such art appears therefore, let us not say childish, for children are wiser, but empty, because of its lack of a true metaphysic. Of this the cries of realism and 'art for art's sake' are evidence enough. A too confident appeal to the so-called facts of nature is to the Indian mind conclusive evidence of superficiality of thought. For the artist above all must this be true, for the first essential of true art is not imitation, but imagination.

What is the ideal of beauty implicit in Indian art? It is a beauty of type, impersonal and aloof. It is not an ideal of varied individual beauty, but of

D

one formalised and rhythmic. The canons insist again and again upon the Ideal as the only true beauty:

"An image whose limbs are made in accordance with the rules laid down in the *sāstras* is beautiful. Some, however, deem that which pleases the fancy to be beautiful; but proportions that differ from those given in the *sāstras* cannot delight the cultured"—(*Sukrācārya*).

The appeal of formalised ideal beauty is for the Indian mind always stronger than that of beauty associated with the accidental and unessential. The beauty of art, whether fictile or literary, is more compelling and deeper than that of nature herself. These pure ideas, thus disentangled from the web of circumstance by art, are less realised and so more suggestive than fact itself. This is the explanation of the passionate love of nature expressed in Indian art and literature, that is yet combined almost with indifference to the beauty, certainly to the 'picturesqueness' of nature herself.

An essential part of the ideal of beauty is restraint in representation:

"The hands and feet should be without veins. The (bones of) the wrist and ankle should not be shown" (*Sukrācārya*). Invisible ankles and wrists are considered beautiful in real life also (see Brihad Samhita, II., xxi., 3, and xxiii., ii.). The sinews also should not be visible. One of the 80 lesser teches of the Buddha was this: 'neither veins nor bones are seen.'

The figure of Avalokitesvara (Plate III.), a small and exquisite bronze of about the Seventh Century, well illustrates this ideal of generalisation and abstraction.

Over-minuteness would be a sacrifice of breadth. It is not for the imager to spend his time in displaying his knowledge or his skill; for over-elaborated detail may destroy rather than heighten

PLATE I

AVALOKITESVARA.

the beauty of the work. The feeling behind this desire for abstract form, and the suppression of unessential detail is exactly analogous to the feeling for pure line and expressive lines in Japanese, and some modern European black and white work. All that is not *necessary* to express the artist's thought is actually a hindrance to its complete expression and reception. But this objection to the laborious realisation of parts of a work of art, must not be confused with the pernicious doctrine of the excellence of unfinished work; it is essential that the artist should always do his best. Oriental art is essentially clear and defined; its mystery does not depend on vagueness.

Adherence to the proportions laid down in the *sāstras* is even inculcated by imprecations:

"If the measurements be out by even half an inch, the result will be loss of wealth, or death"—(*Sāriputra*).

"One who knows amiss his craft....after his death will fall into hell and suffer"—(*Māyāmataya*).

In such phrases we seem to see the framers of the canon, consciously endeavouring to secure the permanence of the tradition in future generations, and amongst ignorant or inferior craftsmen. We shall see later what has been the function of tradition in Indian art. It appears here as an extension in time of the idea of formal beauty and symbolism.

It is not necessary for all art to be beautiful, certainly not pretty. If art is ultimately to 'interpret God to all of you,' it must be now beautiful, now terrible, but always with that living quality which transcends the limited conceptions of beauty and ugliness. The personal God whom alone art can interpret, is in and through all nature; "All this Universe is strung upon Me as gems upon a thread." Nature is sometimes soft and smiling, sometimes also red in tooth and claw; in her both life and death are found. Creation, preservation

D 2

and destruction are equally His work. His images may therefore be beautiful or terrible.

In nature there are three *gunas*, or qualities, *Sattva* (truth), *Rajas* (passion), and *Tamas* (gloom). These qualities are always present in nature; their relative proportion determines the character of any particular subject or object. They must, therefore, enter into all material and conditioned representations, even of Divinity. And so we find a classification of images into three, *sattvik*, *rajasik*, and *tamasik*:

"An image of God, seated self-contained, in the posture of a *yogi*, with hands turned as if granting boon and encouragement to his worshippers, surrounded by praying and worshipping Indra and other gods, is called a *sattvik* image.

"An image seated on a *vāhan*, decked with various ornaments, with hands bearing weapons, as well as granting boon and encouragement, is called a *rajasik* image.

"A *tamasik* image is a terrible armed figure fighting and destroying the demons"—(*Sukrācārya*).

According to Western definitions, art is the imitation of beautiful things,—real or ideal. This view is not different from, but is included in the wider Indian conception of art, which may be defined as the *controlled and rhythmic expression of emotion* (*rasa*). The conception of *rasa* (feeling flavour, burden, passion) is the essential factor in Hindu ideas of æsthetics. The æsthetic faculty is called *ranjini vritti*, 'colouring faculty', because in art all things are conditioned or coloured by *rasa*.*

Now the rasas are nine in number: *sringāra*—Love, with a sex reference, but fundamentally as a spiritual experience; *vira*—the heroic; *karūna*—

* It is not to form and colour, but to feeling that the art consciousness fundamentally relates us. Form, colour and sound are merely means of expression, the immediate beauty of which is very far from representing the whole content of art.

sympathy, compassion; *adbhuta*—wonder; *hasya*—the ridiculous; *bhāyānaka*—fear; *bibhatsa*—disgust; *raudra*—the terrible; and lastly *shānta*—dispassion, peace, the summation and antithesis of the other eight. Of these *sringāra* is called the fundamental (*ādi*) *rasa*. The first and last, which involve the conception of unity, are permanent, the others implying differentiation, impermanent. The first and last correspond nearly to the most ideal Western conception of the 'Beautiful'; they represent the Absolute; but in Indian æsthetic thought, this Absolute or Universal is regarded as Rasa. The difference between Eastern and Western thought is thus less than at first appears; it appears in the greater generalisation of the conception Rasa, as compared with that of Beauty.

We can understand this by a comparison with Greek art and drama. Greek art (*i. e.* classic sculpture—not vase paintings) is limited by the conception of the gods as beautiful Olympians; there is nothing in it like the 'Bacchae' of Euripides. But in Greek drama we find the wonder and mysticism which the art, with all its beauty, lacks. Indian art has the wider content of Greek drama. Curiously enough, however, Indian drama is limited somewhat, as is Greek sculpture, by the idea of pleasure or beauty.

All conceptions of Beauty are coloured by Love; *sringāra* is the *ādi rasa*. All æsthetic delight has its foundation in the Universal and Absolute. But this Absolute—Unity—or Love, is not an abstraction but a Person, God. Thus it becomes clear to us how it is that the highest aim of art, which is the expression of *rasa*, is conceived to be the interpretation and intimation of the Divine, the Ultimate Reality spoken of in the Vedas as Rasa, and apprehended in Vaishnavic thought as Nikhilarasāmrita-murti, the Universal Form of all Emotion and all Bliss.

Ideas of formal beauty identical with those above indicated are also expressed in decorative art. The aim of such art is not, of course, in the same sense consciously religious; the simple expression of delight in cunning workmanship, or of the craftsman's humour, or his fear or his desire, are motifs that inspire the lesser art that belongs to the common things of life. But yet all art is really one, consistent with itself and with life; how should one part of it be fundamentally opposed to another? And so we find in the decorative art of India the same idealism that is inseparable from Indian thought; for art, like religion, is really a way of looking at things, more than anything else.

Eastern decorative art is characterised especially by rhythm, definite form and firm outline. It is the entire lack of these, and particularly of rhythm, in '*l'art nouveau*,' and in 'naturalistic decorative' art generally, which best explains their failure to dignify an object ornamented, or to satisfy the eye or heart.

The love of nature in its infinite beauty and variety has impelled the Oriental craftsman to decorate his handiwork with the forms of the well-known birds and flowers and beasts with which he is most intimate, or which have most appealed to his imagination. But these forms he never represents realistically, they are always memory pictures, combined with fanciful creations of the imagination, into symmetrical and rhythmic ornament.

Take, for example, the treatment of lions in decorative art. Verses of the canon relating to animals often show that the object of the canon has been as much to stimulate imagination, as to define the manner of representation.

"The neigh of a horse is like the sound of a storm, his eyes like the lotus, he is swift as the wind, as stately as a lion, and his gait is the gait of a dancer.

CAPITAL OF ASOKA COLUMN AT SARNĀTH.

"The lion has eyes like those of a hare, a fierce aspect, soft hair long on his chest and under his shoulders, his back is plump like a sheep's, his body is that of a blooded horse, his gait is stately, and his tail long".—(*Sāriputra*).

For comparison I quote another description, from an old Chinese canon:

"With a form like that of a tiger, and with a colour tawny or sometimes blue, the lion is like the *Muku-inu*, a shaggy dog. He has a huge head, hard as bronze, a long tail, forehead firm as iron, hooked fangs, eyes like bended bows, and raised ears; his eyes flash like lightning, and his roar is like thunder."*

Such descriptions throw light on the representation of animals in Oriental decorative art. The artist's lion need be like no lion on earth or in any zoological garden; for he is not illustrating a work on natural history. Freed from such a limitation, he is able to express through his lion the whole theory of his national existence and individual idiosyncracy. Thus has Oriental art been preserved from such paltry and emasculated realism as that of the lions of Trafalgar Square. Contrast the absence of imagination in this handiwork of the English painter of domestic pets, with the vitality of the heraldic lions of Mediæval England, or the lions of Hokusai's 'Daily Exorcisms.' The sculptured lions of Egypt, Assyria, or India (see Plate IV.) are true works of art, for in them we see, not any lion that could to-day be shot or photographed in a desert, but the lion as he existed in the minds of a people, a lion that tells us something of the people who represented him. In such artistic subjectivity lies the significance of Ancient and Eastern decorative art: it is this which gives so much dignity and

* *Quoted in 'The Kokka,' No.* 198, 1906.

value to the lesser arts of India, and separates them so entirely in spirit from the imitative decorative art of modern Europe.

Take Indian jewellery as another illustration of idealism in decorative art. The traditional forms have distinctive names, just as a 'curb bracelet' or a 'gipsy ring' may be spoken of in England. In India the names are usually those of special flowers or fruits, or generic terms for flowers or seeds, as '*rui*-flower thread,' 'coconut-flower garland,' 'petal garland,' 'string of millet grains,' 'ear-flower,' 'hair-flower.' These names are reminiscent of the garlands of real flowers, and the flowers in the hair, that play so important a part in Indian festal dress. These, with the flowers and fruits worn as talismans or as religious symbols, are the prototypes of the flower forms of Indian jewellery, which thus, like all other Indian art, reflects the thought, the life and the history of the people by and for whom it is so beautifully made.

The traditional forms, then, are named after flowers; but it is highly characteristic that the garlands and flowers are in design purely suggestive, not at all imitative of the prototypes. The realism which is so characteristic of nearly all modern Western art, in jewellery producing the unimaginative imitations of flowers, leaves, and animals of the school of Lalique, is never found in Indian design.

The passion for imitation may be taken as direct evidence of the lack of true artistic impulse, which is always a desire, conscious or sub-conscious, to express or manifest Idea. Why indeed imitate where you can never rival? Nor is it by a conscious intellectual effort that a flower is to be conventionalised and made into applied ornament. No Indian craftsman sets a flower before him and worries out of it some sort of ornament by taking thought; his art is more deeply rooted in the national life than that.* If the flower has not meant so much to him that he has already a clear memory picture of its essential characters, he may as well ignore it in his decoration; for a decorative art not intimately related to his own experience, and to that of his fellow men, could have no intrinsic vitality, nor meet with that immediate response which rewards the prophet speaking in a mother-tongue. It is, of course, true that the original memory pictures are handed on as crystallised traditions; yet as long as the art is living, the tradition remains also plastic, and is moulded imperceptibly by successive generations. The force of its appeal is strengthened by the association of ideas,—artistic, emotional and religious. Traditional forms have thus a significance not merely foreign to any imitative art, but dependent on the fact that they represent rather race conceptions, than the ideas of one artist or a single period. They are a vital expression of the race mind: to reject them, and expect great art to live on as before, would be to sever the roots of a forest tree, and still look for flowers and fruit upon its branches.

Consider, also, patterns. To most people patterns mean extremely little; the yare things to be made and cast aside for new, only requiring to be pretty, perhaps only to be fashionable; whereas they are things which live and grow, and which no man can create, all he can do is to use them, and to let them grow. Rhythm and beauty are absorbed and self-existent. The artist is not one who makes, but one who finds.

Every real pattern has a long ancestry and a story to tell. For those that can read its language, even the most strictly decorative art has complex

* The Western craftsman will not recover his power of design until he worships God with flowers; until the sacraments of life are once more made a ritual; nor until he gets back some real superstitions in place of the superstition of 'facts.' Any Catholic would understand this.

and symbolical associations that enhance a thousandfold the significance of its expression, as the complex associations that belong to words, enrich the measured web of spoken verse. This is not, of course, to suggest that such art has a didactic character, but only that it has some meaning and something to say; but if you do not want to listen, it is still as a piece of decoration far better than some new thing that has 'broken with tradition' and is 'original.'

May Heaven preserve us from the decorative art of to-day, that professes to be new and original. The truth is expressed by Ruskin in the following words:

"That virtue of originality that men so strain after is not *newness* (as they vainly think), it is only genuineness; it all depends on this single glorious faculty of getting to the spring of things and working out from that."

Observe that here we have come back to the essentially Indian point of view, getting to the spring of things, and working out from that. You will get all the freshness and individuality you want if you do that. This is to be seen in the vigour and vitality of the design of William Morris, compared with the work of designers who have deliberately striven to be original. Morris tried to do no more than recover the thread of a lost tradition and carry it on; and yet no one could mistake the work of Morris for that of any other man or any other century or country—and is not that originality enough? The one thing essential is imaginative intensity; and with novelty of form, this intensity has little or no connection.

Convention may be defined as the manner of artistic presentation, while tradition stands for a historic continuity in the use of such conventional methods of expression. Many have thought that convention and tradition are the foes of art, and deem the epithets 'conventional and traditional' to be in themselves of the nature of destructive criticism. Convention is conceived of solely as limitation, not as a language and a means of expression. But to one realising what tradition really means, a quite contrary view presents itself; that of the terrible and almost hopeless disadvantage from which art suffers when each artist and each craftsman, or at the best, each little group and school, has first to create a language, before ideas can be expressed in it. For tradition is a wonderful, expressive language, that enables the artist working through it to speak directly to the heart without the necessity for explanation. It is a mother-tongue, every phrase of it rich with the countless shades of meaning read into it by the simple and the great that have made and used it in the past.

It may be said that these principles hold good only in relation to decorative art. Let us then enquire into the place and influence of tradition in the fine art of India. The written traditions, once orally transmitted, consist mainly of memory verses, exactly corresponding to the mnemonic verses of early Indian literature. In both cases the artist, imager or story-teller, had also a fuller and more living tradition, handed down in the schools from generation to generation, enabling him to fill out the meagre details of the written canon. Sometimes, in addition to the verses of the canon, books of mnemonic sketches were in use, and handed down from master to pupil in the same way. These give us an opportunity of more exactly understanding the nature and method of tradition. In Fig. 1 is reproduced from an old Tamil craftsman's sketch book, a figure of Siva as Naṭarāja. In order to understand this, it is necessary first to explain the legend and conception of Siva's appearance as the 'Dancing Lord.' The story is given in the *Koyil*

Purāṇam, and is familiar to all Saivites. Siva appeared in disguise amongst a congregation of ten thousand sages, and in the course of disputation, confuted them and so angered them thereby, that they endeavoured by incantations to destroy Him. A fierce tiger was created in sacrificial flames, and rushed upon Him; but smiling gently, He seized it with His sacred hands, and with the nail of His little finger stripped off its skin, which He wrapped about Himself as if it had been a silken cloth. Undiscouraged by failure, the sages renewed their offerings, and there was produced a monstrous serpent, which He seized and wreathed about His neck. Then He began to dance; but there rushed upon Him a last monster in the shape of a hideous malignant dwarf. Upon him the God pressed the tip of His foot, and broke the creature's back, so that it writhed upon the ground; and so, His last foe prostrate, Siva resumed the dance of which the gods were witnesses. A modern interpretation of this legend explains that He wraps about Him, as a garment, the tiger fury of human passion; the guile and malice of mankind He wears as a necklace, and beneath His feet is for ever crushed the embodiment

Fig. 1. Naṭarāja, "dancer in the hall of Southern Tillai."—(Manikka Vacagar) from a Tamil craftsman's notebook (early XIXth century).

of evil. More characteristic of Indian thought is the symbolism, in terms of the marvellous grace and rhythm of Indian dancing, the effortless ease with which the God in His grace supports the cosmos; it is His sport. The five acts of creation, preservation, destruction, embodiment and gracious release are His ceaseless mystic dance. In sacred Tillai, the 'New Jerusalem,' the dance shall be revealed; and Tillai is the very centre of the Universe, that is, His dance is within the cosmos and the soul.*

"Our God," says a Tamil text, "is the Dancer Who like the heat latent in firewood diffuses His Power in Mind and matter and makes them dance in their turn." Sivan here is one with Eros Protogonos, Lord of Life and Death, of whom Lucian spoke when he said, "It would seem that dancing came into being at the beginning of all things, and was brought to light together with Eros, that ancient one, for we see this primæval dancing clearly set forth in the choral dance of the constellations, and in the planets and fixed stars, their interweaving and interchange and orderly harmony."

The necessity for such an explanation emphasizes the apparent difficulty of understanding Indian art; but it must be remembered that the element of strangeness in Indian art is not there for its makers and those for whom they worked; it speaks, as all great national art must speak, in a language of its own, and it is evident that the grammar of this art language must be understood before the message can be appreciated, or the mind left free to consider what shall be its estimate of the artistic qualities of a work before it.

Here then is a rough sketch, drawn by an ordinary craftsman, and representing very fairly just that amount of guidance which tradition some-

* *Pope, 'Tiruvāçagam.' p.* LXIII.; *'Nallasawmi Pillai, 'Sivagnana Botham,' Madras,* 1895, *p.* 74.

what precisely hands on for the behoof of each succeeding generation of imagers. This conception is fairly often met with in Southern India, sculptured in stone or cast in bronze. Some of these representations have no especial artistic excellence; but so subjective is appreciation of art, so dependent on qualities belonging entirely to the beholder, and transferred by him into the object before him, that the symbolic and religious aim is still attained. Such is one of the functions of tradition, making it possible for ordinary craftsmen to work acceptably within its limits, and avoiding all danger of the great and sacred subjects being treated with loss of dignity or reverence. But tradition has another aspect, as enabling the great artist, the man of genius, to say, in the language understanded of the people, all that there is in him to express.

A bronze figure of Natarāja is shown in Plate I.; it represents a figure in the Madras Museum, perhaps of the seventeenth century, probably older. It would be superfluous to praise in detail this beautiful figure; it is so alive, and yet so balanced, so powerful and yet so effortless. There is here realism for the realist, but realism that is due to keenness of memory for familiar things, not to their imitation. The imager grew up under the shadow of a Sivan temple in one of the great cathedral cities of the South; perhaps Tanjore; he had worked with his father at the columns of the Thousand Pillared Hall at Madura, and later at the Choultry, when all the craftsmen of Southern India flocked to carry out the great buildings of Tirumala Nāyaka; himself a Saivite, he knew all its familiar ritual, and day after day had seen the dancing of the *devadāsīs* before the shrine, perhaps in his youth had been the lover of one, more skilled and graceful than the rest; and all his memories of rhythmic dance, and mingled devotion for *devadāsī* and for Deity, he expressed in the

PLATE V.

DHYĀNI BUDDHA.

grace and beauty of this dancing Siva. For so are religion and culture, life and art, bound up together in the web of Indian life. Is the tradition that links that art to life of little value, or less than none, to the great genius? Shall he reject the imagery ready to his hand, because it is not new and unfamiliar? Look well at the figure, with its first and simplest motif of victory over evil; observe the ring of flaming fire, the aura of His glory; the four hands with the elaborate symbolism of their attitude; the ganges and crescent moon in His hair; the fluttering *angavastiram*, and the serpent garland, and think whether any individual artist, creating his own convention and inventing newer symbolisms, could speak thus to the hearts of men, amongst whom the story of Siva's dance is a gospel and a cradle tale.

The seated Buddha (Plate V.) is a more familiar type. Here, too, convention and tradition are held to fetter artistic imagination. Indian art is sometimes condemned for showing no development, because there is, or is supposed to be, no difference in artistic conception between a Buddha of the first century and one of the nineteenth. It is, of course, not quite true that there is no development, in the sense that the work of each period is altogether uncharacterised; for those who know something of Indian art are able to estimate with some confidence the century to which a statue belongs. But it is true that the conception is really the same; the mistake lies in thinking this an artistic weakness. It is an expression of the fact that the Indian ideal has not changed. What is that ideal so passionately desired? It is one-pointedness, same-sightedness, control: little by little to control the fickle and unsteady mind; little by little to win stillness, to rein in, not merely the senses, but the mind, that is as hard to check as is the wind. As a lamp that flickers not in a windless spot, so is the mind to be at rest. Only by constant labour and passionlessness are this peace and the realization that is its end to be attained. What is the attitude of mind and body of one that seeks it? He shall be seated like the image, for that posture once acquired, is one of perfectly bodily equipoise.

"He shall seat himself with thought intent and the workings of mind and sense instruments restrained, for purification of spirit labour on the *yoga*.

"Firm, holding body, head, and neck in unmoving equipoise, gazing on the end of his nose, and looking not round about him.

"Calm of spirit, void of fear, abiding under the vow of chastity, with mind restrained and thought set on Me, so shall he sit that is under the Rule, given over unto Me.

"In this wise the *yogi* . . . comes to the peace that ends in *nirvāna* and that abides in Me"—(*Bhagavad Gītā*, *VI.*, 12-15).

How then should the greatest of India's teachers be represented in art? How otherwise than seated in this posture that is in the heart of India associated with every striving after the great Ideal, and in which the Buddha himself was seated on the night when the attacks of Māra were for ever foiled, and that insight came at last, to gain which the Buddha had in countless lives sacrificed his body 'for the sake of creatures'? It was the greatest moment in India's spiritual history; and as it lives in the race-memory, so is it of necessity presented in the race-art.

It is usual nowadays to demand what is called originality in works of art, to ask that they shall bear not only the artist's name, but the impress of his individuality, he is expected to 'be himself,' 'break away from tradition' and the like. Only with such work, do men now associate that emotional intensity that men less feverishly seeking for some new thing, associated of old with the retelling of a twice-told tale.

For these nameless artists, the one great thing was not so much to express themselves in their work, but to tell the great thing itself, that meant so much to them and which it was theirs to re-express. Not by their names do we remember them. Theirs is an immortality more perfect, because more impersonal. Art that is altogether original can never be truly great. How could one man's labour rival the results of centuries of race-imagining? The true material of art must ever be that which has already commanded the hearts of men rather than any fancy of the passing hour.

Such, then, have been the aims and method of Indian Art in the past. Two tendencies are manifested in the Indian art of to-day, the one inspired by the technical achievement of the modern West, the other by the spiritual idealism of the East. The former has swept away both the beauty and the limitation of the old tradition. The latter has but newly found expression; yet if the greatest art is always both National and Religious (and how empty any other art must be), it is there alone that we see the beginnings of a new and greater art, that shall fulfil and not destroy the past. When a living Indian culture arises out of the wreck of the past and the struggle of the present, a new tradition will be born, and new vision find expression in the language of form and colour no less than in that of words and rhythm. The people to whom the great conceptions came are still the Indian people, and, when life is strong in them again, strong also will be their art. It may well be that the fruit of a deeper national life, a wider culture, and a profounder love, will be an art greater than any of the past. But this can only be through growth and development, not by a sudden rejection of the past. A particular convention is the characteristic

E

expression of a period, the product of particular conditions; it resumes the historic evolution of the national culture. The convention of the future must be similarly related to the national life. We stand in relation both to past and future; in the past we made the present, the future we are moulding now, and our duty to this future is that we should enrich, not destroy, the inheritance that is not India's alone, but the inheritance of all humanity.

CHAPTER V.

Art and Yoga in India.

IN these notes it is proposed briefly to indicate the connection between art and yoga in India. The yoga philosophy of India is the applied science of psychology, and has naturally, as such, profoundly influenced the whole development of Indian culture. Yoga is the science of the mind, particularly in relation to concentration and attention, and, though in its highest and most usual sense the aim of union of the self with the Self is implied, its methods are perfectly general and applicable to every kind of mental activity.

These methods are briefly indicated in Patanjali, III, 1-4. "Attention (*dharana*) is the fixing of the mind in a given place: contemplation (*dhyāna*) consists in the uninterrupted current of cognition thereof: the same shining on the object only, and emptied of all self-reference, is rapture (*samādhi*). These three together constitute identification of subject with object (*sanyama*)."

Now Indian art stands related to yoga in three ways: In respect of the Divine Ideal,* characteristic methods, and ultimate purpose. The present notes deal chiefly with the methods and briefly with the aims of Indian art. The following summary of an imager's ritual will illustrate their yogic character. The details are taken from Tāntric books of about the 12th century, summarised by M. Foucher in his

* See Ch. IV. *supra*, and Mr. E. B. Havell's "Indian Sculpture and Painting."

E 2

'Iconographic Bouddhique' (Part II). The methods are no doubt much older than the extant literature, in which moreover they are presented perhaps in a somewhat rigid and extreme form. Indeed, adherence to the letter rather than to the spirit of these formulas may have contributed to the ultimate decline of the very art originally developed on the lines of the essential truths underlying them. However that may be, we are able to gain from these texts a remarkable insight into the relations of art and yoga.

The artist then, or magician (*sādhaka*, *mantrin* or *yogin*) as he is called, is to proceed to a solitary place, after purificatory ablutions, and wearing newly-washed garments. There he is to perform the 'Seven-fold office' beginning with the invocation of the hosts of Buddhas and Bodhisattvas in the open space before him, and the offering to them of real or imaginary flowers, and ending with a dedication of the merit acquired, to the welfare of all beings. Then he has to realise in thought the four infinite qualities (love, compassion, sympathy, same-sightedness). Then he must meditate on the original purity of the first principles of things, and on (what comes to the same thing) their emptiness or absolute non-existence. "By the fire of the idea of emptiness, it is said, there are destroyed beyond recovery the five elements" which compose the individual consciousness. Only when the personality of the individual is thus set aside is he able to invoke the divinity desired to be represented, and to attain identity with this divinity, which last condition is strictly enjoined. For complete comprehension is only possible when the consciousness is thus identified with an object of cognition. All this takes place in the imagination. The divinity appears 'like a reflection' or 'as in a dream.' Very rarely indeed is any drawing made use of, even in the most complicated conceptions, where the principal personage is surrounded by disciples in the centre of a *mandala.* It is only when the mental image is thus defined that the artist begins to mould or paint.

Another analogy between art and yoga is found in a reliance upon knowledge obtained in sleep or dreams. One method of overcoming obstacles to yoga, says Patanjali, is by "dwelling on knowledge that presents itself in dream or sleep." Just this knowledge is referred to in the Agni Purāna (Ch. 43), where the imager is instructed, on the night before beginning his work, and after ceremonial purification, to pray: "O thou Lord of all gods, teach me in dreams how to carry out all the work I have in my mind."

The same principles hold good in secular art. Everything is painted or carved out of the artist's own head, (whence, as Burne-Jones truly said, all pictures ought to come) not from any visible model posing before him. Even 'drawing from nature' means 'drawing from memory.' And this applies likewise to the modern school of Bengali painting, which represents a return to Indian idealism, largely inspired by the painting of the Moghal period.

It will be seen that the artistic method is thus practically identical with the method of personal devotion—meditation on and self-identification with the mentally conceived form of the *Ishṭa Devatā.* And what a training such a method of worship provides for the imagination of the artist! For the true artist is not he who 'composes' a picture, but he who 'sees' it. This apprehension of ideas apparently arriving from outside the ordinary consciousness is 'inspiration,' the real characteristic of genius. This is well expressed in the Persian distinction between *āward* (to bring), applied to rhyming and composition by one's own personal effort, and *āmad* (to come), applied to writing with spontaneous flow of thought, inspiration. Observe how *Vyāsa* demanded of *Ganesha* that he should write down his slokas without stopping. A public speaker is at his best when he 'forgets himself'; and if the thread of his discourse is broken, he becomes self-conscious, and the remainder of his speech may be spoilt. Many speakers too, could not repeat or remember afterwards, 'in cold blood,' the words they used when 'carried away' by the temporary stimulus. Very significant is the way in which Srī Krishna, when asked to repeat the *gītā* after the battle, was not able to do so—he had *forgotten* it. 'We cannot kindle when we will the fire that in the soul resides'; or would it be truer to say that in some measure we can, when by 'standing still from self-thinking and self-willing' (Behmen) room is left for greater things, from which at ordinary times self-consciousness divides us?

Such is the teaching of yoga, and such also is the meaning of art.

> "Of beauty they have sung in every age
> He who perceives it is *from himself* set free."

The Indian conception of the artistic imagination, whether in artist or spectator, is akin to that of religious ecstasy. The great philosopher Abhinavaguptapādācarya explains that, when we enjoy a beautiful piece of poetry, we realise our own higher self. What is called *bhoga* (delight) is nothing but the revelation of our own higher nature conditioned by *sattva* (truth), and previously obscured by *rajas* (selfish activity) and *tamas* (inertness). Since our higher nature is essentially blissful, the delight we experience is comparable to Brahmanic bliss.*

This view is akin to that of the neo-Platonists. According to Plotinus: "The explanation of delight in sensible beauty, so far as it can be explained, is

* Prof. V. V. Sovani, Vedic Mag. Vol. II, No. 10.

that when the soul perceives something akin to its own nature it feels joy in it." Good and beauty in themselves—Sattva and Rasa—are the principle to which souls naturally aspire. "This is to be reached by closing the eyes to common sights and arousing another power of vision which all have, but few make use of." *

Another parallel is afforded by the lives of saints and heroes. "Christ and his disciples were artists inasmuch as their speech and action were penetrated by the rapture of an inward vision. Art and religion are a motion of the soul, or self-forgetfulness of the individual before the universal life. The artist sees or half sees a vision, which, though it is yet formless, though as yet he has not realised it or made it his own, draws him from himself." †

The true significance of art, in a view of life which values all things solely in so far as they conduce to the attainment of moksha,‡ lies in the self-forgetfulness and Self-realisation which it involves alike for artist and spectator.

It is said that men dread Pantheism, not because they are afraid of losing God, but because they fear to lose themselves. This is the secret of the Western shrinking from those Oriental religions which are supposed to preach 'extinction' as the desired goal. But only he that will lose his life shall save it; and he that would save his life shall lose it. Compare the consciousness of a savage with that of a refined and cultured man. Most of the savage's self-consciousness, ideas of good, self-protection, hunting and fighting, have for the other passed into the region of sub-consciousness, accessible at will, but no longer filling the whole circle

* Whitaker, 'The Neo-Platonists' (Plotinus, Enn I., 6, 8).

† B. de Selincourt, 'Hibbert Journal,' Jan. 1907.

‡ *Moksha*—the goal of all religion, self-realisation, *i.e.* passing from the superficial ego, empirical and sensational in consciousness, to the Self seated in the heart of all things.

of the mind. The ordinary consciousness of the cultured man, on the other hand, is composed of thoughts outside the range of the savage mind, and at the same time, as we have said, relegates ideas of the latter to the region of sub-consciousness. Yet even the savage too may have intuitions of these higher things; but he may hardly be able to explain them except in terms of negation of ordinary experience. Just so the higher man is lifted at times by the exaltation of love, by art, by philosophy, or by deliberate effort (*yoga*) above *his* ordinary consciousness. And this is not a loss—it is an infinite gain. It is not extinction but realisation. But from the standpoint of the empirical consciousness it has often to be described only in terms of negation.

According to Plato, the things we see about us are but the shadows of real things we do not see. Just so it is imagined by the Indian mind that the life of a Hindu, his art and architecture, and music are, as it were, shadows or echoes of realities elsewhere. "Send to the world of the devas," said the royal builder, "and procure for me a plan of their palace."

Deva nāgari, 'Sanskrit,' is in a very liberal sense the language of the gods. The Hindu temple and its ritual are, as it were, reflections of the actual adoration of Mahadev or Kailas. There are manifest the realities which Plato called Ideas, whose shadows only are seen by mortal men. But the true artist is not mortal, he is a 'hero,' one who has eyes to see and ears to hear. It is for him to make manifest to us what he himself has seen, to make the ideal real, to lift us thereby, if only for a moment, to the level of his truer vision. Can we wonder that architecture so imagined is both grand and beautiful, or can such conceptions fail to be reflected in the dignity and serenity of life itself? Under such conditions the builder is not an individual expressing individual whims, but a part of the

Universe, giving expression to the ideals of its own beauty, rhythm and unchanging law.

Plato conceived only of an imitative art, a shadow of the shadows: he did not imagine the possibility of the artist's direct approach by intuition to the more profound reality. He perceived that the art of his own time was not in the highest sense religious, he saw that it was built on no deep metaphysic. Greek art—*i.e.* classic Greek sculpture—has no touch of mysticism. It may be that Plato would have distrusted equally any art that had. However that may be, he gives no sign of recognition of the possibility of a spiritually idealistic art such as that of Egypt, India, or Mediæval Europe.

As the ideal, so, as nearly as possible, the real—this is the fundamental principle through which alone Indian culture can be understood or judged. The great civilising force called Hinduism is a literal attempt to realise the kingdom of heaven on earth. This is the explanation of religious art traditions, of the continuity in Indian music, architecture and ritual. Those for whom the Ideal was a matter of actual experience, who saw and heard the true realities and revealed them to less gifted men, willed that they should not be forgotten.

It is for us, not to follow after our own vain imaginings in art or life, not even—though this might well content us—to follow blindly on the lines laid down by the ancient shapers of Indian culture; but to so refine ourselves that we may see and hear again the true realities and re-express them in terms of our present consciousness.

The Indian artist set himself deliberately to make the unseen more real than the seen. And by strange good fortune he was therein in the perfect sympathy and understanding of those for whom he worked; for it was said in India, that only those 'devoid of Reason' think of Him, the unmanifest, as having manifestation, knowing not the reality that is hidden by His *yoga māyā*.

Asia, indeed, has been almost continuously free from the, to her, childish conception that the highest aim of art lies in the successful imitation of nature. It has been left for modern Europe to follow the example of Pheidias in an endeavour rather to reproduce than to understand. Europe, though temporarily freed in Gothic art from the purely physical idealism of Greek, fell with the Renaissance once more under the sway of its unsatisfying intellectualism ; the logical conclusion follows in the modern complete subjection of art to science. Corrupted by science, as has been truly said, the Western mind now demands of artists, not great ideas, imagination, fancy, tenderness, but what it calls 'realism,' little dreaming how far removed this may be from 'truth.' Modern art is primarily an intellectual process. The historical or religious painter has become an archæologist—and this, forsooth, is what we mean by 'faithfulness.' Not thus did the great painters of mediæval Italy or of China, or the sculptors of Egypt or of India work. They indeed sought truth, but they sought it where alone it is to be found, within. We talk of the faithful presentation of life: but what is life? We do not realise that these men lived in a world more real and wonderful than any that we know. That life was the life they represented for us. Because we know it not we call it unreal. It is what men dream, not anything they do, that is real. Infinitely greater is thought than action. The dreams of a race, the thoughts of God, and not the acts of the bodies of individuals are the true realities of art. Art is not an analysis of things, but their synthesis, a revelation of the reality enduring behind the evanescent, a revelation above all of love, that is Unity.

The most general definition of art is the 'rhythmic expression and suggestion of controlled emotion' (*rasa*). Art that is uncoloured by *rasa** is no longer art, but science. How then are we to judge of art? Not surely as we judge of empirical science, by the test of accuracy of observation. The true basis of art criticism is embodied in the pregnant words of Leonardo da Vinci: "That drawing is best which best expresses the passion that animates the figure." 'Passion' is here the exact equivalent of '*rasa*.' We do wrong to demand of the artist that he should compete with the appliances of science—we should ask from him not 'realism,' but truth, sincerity, imagination and emotion! How far second to these are the standards of archæological and anatomical accuracy, by reference to which the modern public tests a work of art! This modern public, Indian or English, with its complacent ignorance, provides a mental atmosphere which is —with rare exceptions of men who are able definitely to live in a world of their own—quite fatal to the possibility of any real art.

The keynote of all great art, no less than of *yoga*, is selflessness. And yet originality is actually thought of by the modern art student as a duty! He loves to be described as 'seeing things with his own eyes,' as 'emancipated from the last traces of tradition.' He does not long to make himself a medium of expression of the spirit of his race, but to impress his own more limited individuality upon the work of his hand; and he would shrink in horror from the idea of leaving his work unsigned, of being but a nameless unit in a group of workers inspired by one ideal. Each modern artist seeks to invent

* Dispassion is included under *rasa*. Perfect balance (same-sightedness) is not the absence of emotion, but the transcending of emotions. In the Buddha type, dispassion itself is the 'passion that animates the figure.'

for himself a new artistic Esperanto, unmistakably his and his alone. The result of this artistic egoism is a corresponding barrenness: for isolation is limitation. In how different a spirit the great sculptors and painters and writers of old have worked! Nearly all great things are impersonal.

Who wrote the Mahābhārata? Vyāsa, 'the compiler.' Who were the authors of the Vedas? 'Rishis' 'heard' them. Who first 'saw' the great cat-gods of Egypt, the Chinese dragon, or the dance of Sivan? Who carved the images at Chartres? Who shaped the Keltic otherworlds or dreamed of that Himālayan forest of Broceliande that is the innermost sanctuary of the Land of Gods? Not one of these is known to us by name, nor are the records of their lives detailed in interesting biographies.

To seek after originality, as Novalis truly perceived, is egoism. How much greater to stand aside from this 'gross egoism,' more than content if by intensity of imagination we too can grasp and represent some shadow of the great realities that artists in all ages have seen and heard. And this intensity of imagination is true inspiration (in-breathing); it is the setting aside of the lower self, and the inflow of a larger self, in touch with a more real reality. And this, once more, is *yoga:* to stand still from self-willing and self-thinking; from a part to become the whole; from dreams to awaken to the truth behind them.

Such then are some aspects of the relation between art and yoga in India. It has been said that when a new inspiration comes into Western art, it will come again from the East. This I believe. It is the lack of a metaphysic that makes so much of modern art uninteresting and monotonous. Art which has no concern with the subjective life, with things unseen that are more real than those that are called real, is little more than science.

It may be that the influence of the East will restore to the world some measure of the romance and beauty that commerce and materialism have taken away. This is, indeed, the only hope; for it is of little use to be more ingenious than our forefathers if our real life is smaller. The greatness of men lies in their beliefs, not in the multiplicity of things they disbelieve. Religion, for India, is personal experience of the supersensual within one's own consciousness—Thou art That; Thou art the Buddha; The Kingdom of Heaven is within you. It is part of the message of the East that this inward vision, this divine imagination, is essential to all real art; that the impersonal beauty of a type is greater far than the representation of the transitory and individual.

And if we desire to understand why this ideal art is greater than any imitation of the beauty of nature as we see it with physical eyes, we shall find that it is because this ideal art, by reason of the element of timelessness and universality in its presentation, frees us most from self, raising us for a time to the plane of æsthetic contemplation, which the artist himself attained when he first saw the picture itself. To understand a poem or a picture, you must, however dimly, enter into the spiritual atmosphere in which it was conceived; "to read poetry, you must be a poet; to see a picture, you must be an artist." It is this demand of ideal art upon the spectator's own imagination which is the secret of its power, and which explains the Indian saying, that the image of a God, even though misshapen, is better than the image of a man, however beautiful. Realistic, and fully realised, art is finite, and carries the spectator nowhither that he was not already; ideal and suggestive art is infinite and may carry the true spectator as far as, nay farther than, the artist himself has gone. I say the true spectator, because there is as much distinction of spectators as of artists, and for both in almost equal measure is true imagination needed. It is in this power of carrying the spectator away from his empirical and sensational self, by self-forgetfulness, some little way towards that higher 'Self that is seated in the heart of all things,' that there lies the explanation of the truth, that artists are amongst the prophets.

CHAPTER VI.

The Influence of Modern Europe on Indian Art.

"It is on the architecture of to-day that the preservation of Indian Art in any semblance of healthy life now hinges."

J. L. KIPLING, *Journal of Indian Art*, VOL. I.

THE fate of Indian decorative art in modern times needs no elaborate demonstration. A comparison of the manufactures of a hundred, or even fifty, years ago, as seen in the museums of Europe and India, with the productions of to-day, reveals a degradation in quality of material and design which it would be practically impossible to exaggerate. There is no more depressing aspect of present day conditions than the universal decline of taste in India, from the Raja, whose palace, built by the London upholsterer* or imitated from some European building,† is furnished with vulgar superfluity and uncomfortable grandeur, to the peasant clothed in Manchester cottons of appalling hue and meaningless design. The Delhi exhibition was a sufficient revelation of the extent to which the degradation has advanced. References to it appear on every page of books like Sir George Birdwood's 'Industrial Arts of India,' Sir George Watt's 'Indian Art at Delhi,' and amongst the incidental references of almost every traveller and writer on Indian

* Like one now in progress, being made by a firm of upholsterers in London for the ruler of a small State in the Punjab, at a cost of 35 lacs.

† Like a well-known palace in Calcutta a copy of Windsor palace.

matters. In 1879 an address to Sir George Birdwood, signed by William Morris, Edward Burne-Jones, Monier Williams, J. E. Millais, Edwin Arnold, Walter Crane and others spoke of "the rapid deterioration that has of late befallen the great historical arts of India." They further remarked that "goods which ought to be common in the market are now becoming rare treasures for museums, or the cabinets of rich men." Let us examine a few instances of this degeneration, selected from various authorities.

"The carpets of Masulipatam were formerly among the finest produced in India, but of late years have also been corrupted by the European, chiefly English, demand for them. The English importers insisted on supplying the weavers with cheaper materials, and we now find that these carpets are invariably backed with English twine. The spell of the tradition thus broken, one innovation after another was introduced into the manufacture. The designs, which of old were full of beautiful detail, and more varied than now in range and scheme of colouring, were surrounded by a delicate outline suggested as to tint by a harmonising contrast with the colours with which it was in contact. But the necessity for cheap and speedily executed carpets for the English market has led to the abandonment of this essential detail in all Indian ornamentation. Crude inharmonious masses of unmeaning form now mark the spots where formerly varied, interesting, and beautiful designs blossomed as delicately as the first flowers of spring: and these once glorious carpets of Masulipatam have sunk to a mockery and travesty of their former selves." (Sir George Birdwood, 1880).

The following quotation from Sir George Watt's 'Indian Art at Delhi' illustrates the nature of the process now taking place throughout the East:

"While examining a large series of old designs, one of the chief kinkhab manufacturers expressed amusement at the interest shown in worthless old mica sketches, long out of fashion. He explained that he possessed a book of great value from which all his most successful designs had, for some years past, been taken. On being desired to show this treasured pattern book he produced a sample book of English wall papers. . . . . This at once explained the monstrous degeneration perceived in the Benares kinkhabs. . . . . . not in Benares only, but throughout India the fine old art designs that have been attained after centuries of evolution are being abandoned and models utterly unsuited and far inferior artistically are being substituted. The writer can confidently affirm that he found in at least 50 per cent. of the important silversmiths' workshops of India the illustrated trade catalogues of European firms and stores being employed as the pattern books upon which their silver plate was being modelled."

The same is true of Ceylon, where Western influence is stronger; every jeweller uses European trade catalogues; it is now the fashion to melt down old jewellery, the most beautiful in design and perfect in workmanship, in order to have copies made of Birmingham designs which a machine has already reproduced a thousand times (the people want, in their own words, "improved jewellery;" but they will find it only where they will last of all turn for it, and then too late, in the workshop of the hereditary craftsman). To take other examples; of Benares brass work—by which Indian art is typically represented to the tourist mind—only two pieces were good enough to show at the Delhi exhibition.

"All but one or two pieces were bad in design and worse in execution. They had departed from the fine old patterns that made Benares famous for its brass wares, most being poor imitations of swami work or of Poona copper ware. Many were in European shapes and purposes." (Sir G. Watt.)

Enamelling has been called the master craft of India; of the most famous centre Sir George Watt remarks:—

"Formerly every attention was given to effect, and a background or field colour was regularly employed, most frequently a rich creamy white. Within the past few decades this has been discontinued, and complex and intricate designs substituted in which it can hardly be said there is a field colour at all. The result is distinctly inferior and may be described as garish rather than artistic. The utilitarian spirit of the times is also marked by the production of a large assortment of sleeve links, lockets, bracelets, brooches and the like, and the decoration of the backs of pieces of jewellery, in place of

F

enamelling, being the chief ornamentation of charms, sword-hilts, plates, etc., as in former times."

Notice particularly the degradation of the art, from its application to objects entering into the serious life of the people of the country, to trivial objects intended mainly for the passing tourist.

Taste in dyed and printed textiles has declined enormously. Perhaps the most glaring example known to me is the replacement of beautiful Indian printed cottons in Madras, by cheaper products of Manchester, having greatly degraded imitations of Indian ornament, or perfectly meaningless decoration such as rows of bicycles, or pictures of banknotes. Some of these have been published as an object lesson, in contrast with Indian prints.* It has been well remarked that such monstrosities are an insult to European knowledge and an outrage on Indian art. Yet I have known educated Indians defend their use on the ground that Indians 'cannot be expected to keep to one pattern always,' and that 'if it is right for Europeans to admire Indian patterns, why is it not right for Indians to make use of European forms?' In the same way, it is sometimes asked why Indians should not copy modern Western, classical, or any forms of architecture that may please them, with the suggestion that the European advice to build in an Indian style is merely the result of a particular fancy, and that there can be no real guiding principle in such matters. Only a century of education, entirely false in aims and method, could have produced such a result as this. Those who gave and those who accepted that education are equally at fault.

In illustration of architectural degeneration, a few quotations will suffice.

"The modern palaces of the Nawabs of the Carnatic, of the Rajas of Ramnad or Travancore, are all in the bastard Italian style, adopted by the Nawabs of Lucknow and the

* Journal of Indian Art, 1897.

Babus of Calcutta. Sometimes, it must be confessed, the buildings are imposing from their mass, and picturesque from their variety of outline, but the details are always detestable, first from being bad copies of a style that was not understood or appreciated, but also generally from their being unsuited for the use to which they were applied. To these defects it must be added, that the whole style is generally characterised by a vulgarity it is difficult to understand in a people who have generally shown themselves capable of so much refinement in former times."*

A Buddhist building lately erected in Colombo, is thus described by a local paper: "The building is a very pretty structure, a vaulted roof with a fine dome, gothic windows, doors and a porch, with parapet battlements of classic design, being very effective." This is a typical illustration of Mr. Growse's statement† that in India "the essence of European architecture is supposed to consist in a reckless disregard of all recognized canons of ornament and proportion."

It would be easy to multiply examples of the degeneration of Indian crafts, but, as the fact is generally admitted, it will be more profitable to consider the causes of this degeneration and the possibilities of arresting it. The causes fall into two groups, external and internal, very closely related, it is true, but for convenience considered separately. To take the external first, we have to consider chiefly the attitude of the British Government in India and in England, the influence of the general export demand, the tourist demand, and the influence of the personal example of Europeans in India. We meet first with the deliberate discouragement of Indian production where it in any way competed with English, and sometimes even where it did not. The first result of British trade with India was to open to India a new market for her

* Ferguson, 'Indian and Eastern Architecture,' 1899 ed., p. 385.

† Journal of Indian Art, Vol. I, 'Indian Architecture To-day,' by J. L. Kipling, p. 3.

textiles in particular. But when it was found possible to manufacture goods of the same character in England,

"endeavours were made, which were fatally successful, to repress Indian manufactures and to extend British manufactures. The import of Indian goods to Europe was repressed by prohibitive duties; the export of British goods to India was encouraged by almost nominal duties. . . In 1816-17 'India not only clothed the whole of that vast population, but exported £1,659,438 worth of goods.' Thirty years later the whole of this export had disappeared, and India imported four millions sterling of cotton goods. . . . . When Queen Victoria ascended the throne in 1837, the evil had been done. But nevertheless there was no relaxation in the policy pursued before. Indian silk hand-kerchiefs had still a sale in Europe; and a high duty on manufactured silk was maintained. Parliament enquired 'how cotton could be grown in India for British looms,' not how Indian looms could be improved. Select committees tried to find out how British manufactures could find a sale in India, not how Indian manufactures could be revived. . . . . During a century and a half the commercial policy of the British rulers of India has been determined, not by the interests of Indian manufacturers, but by those of British manufacturers. The vast quantities of manufactured goods which were exported from India by the Portuguese and Dutch, by Arab and British merchants, in the seventeenth and eighteenth centuries, have disappeared."—(Romesh Dutt).

The same policy has been maintained until a later period. As late as 1905, Mr. Pennington reviewing the book from which I have just quoted, could say:—

"One cannot read such an indictment of England by one of her most capable Indian officials without a feeling of humiliation. . . . . The quite recent story of the imposition of an excise duty on Indian goods which did not compete at all with any Lancashire goods and yet affected seriously the rival mills of India, is a disgrace to Lancashire as well as to the English Government. It is quite certain that if India had as many votes as even the single county of Lancashire, that scandalous duty would never have been imposed. When shall we get to govern us, 'men of truth, hating unjust gain.'?"

Mr. J. Nisbet, writing in the 'Nineteenth Century' for November, 1908, repeats the same well-known facts:—

"As regards Swadeshi, certainly so far as fiscal matters are concerned, the history of the Indian tariff under Crown Government has been one long and almost continuous betrayal of Indian interests in order to win the Lancashire vote for party purposes."

Here is the result of such an attitude.

"The weavers of India were, until recently, a very prosperous class, but the importation of machine-made piece-goods from Manchester has, of late, thrown many thousands of them out of employ. These dragged on a life of poverty for some years, and at last either died of semi-starvation, or were forced by necessity to become menial servants or tillers of the soil."—J. N. Bhattacharya, 'Hindu Castes and Sects.'

These disastrous results have been often enough insisted on by Indians, but from an economic point of view only, it being supposed that, if the weavers and dyers could take to other employment, and if the trade in textiles could be restored to India by the establishment of flourishing mills in towns, the evil would be ended. The disaster is more serious far than that; for you might take as tribute from every weaver half his earnings and still leave to the country his technical capacity, and, a greater thing still, his art knowledge, his power of applying to the productions of his loom the traditional ornament which is still a live expressive thing, embodying the hope of the past and with an ever fresh message to the future; but if you so disorganize society as to make it impossible for him to live at all by weaving —when English manufactures "successfully contest the village weaver's market"—you destroy, not merely the national wealth, but also the national culture.

Let us turn to the direct influence of the British Government in India itself.

"The worst mischief" says Sir George Birdwood, "is perhaps done by the architecture foisted on the country by the Government of India, which being the architecture of the State, is naturally thought to be worthy of all imitation. The Nawab of Bahawalpur was installed the other day on the throne of his ancestors, and in anticipation of the auspicious event, the Indian Government built him a palace, which is the ghastliest piece of bare classicalism it is possible to imagine, even with so many examples before us in this country of the dissenting chapels and vestry halls of the last century. And now Holkar, in obvious emulation of this preposterous production, is building for himself a vast Italian palace at Indore, which is to cost many lakhs of rupees, and will be like Trentham, or Buckingham Palace, or anything else in the world but a habitation meet for kings. This sort of thing has been going on all over India ever since the establishment of the British peace."

Just how the process is carried on in detail is explained by Mr. Havell in an article entitled 'Indian Administration' in the 'Nineteenth Century' for June, 1907.*

As an example of Government at its best I give the following details of endeavour to build in the national style, in a particular case in Ceylon. Needless to say traditional craftsmen were not employed.

The building referred to is a memorial rest house at Ruvanvella. The moulding round the wall, a few feet from the floor, instead of forming an actual part of the wall, as in all old work, consists entirely of plaster applied to the surface of the wall, and is already breaking away. But perhaps the worst feature is a part of the doors. The contractor has remarked the massive arched lintel of a Kandyan door, and by way of imitation, has fastened on to each half of the double door a half sham lintel, so that when the doors are closed, it would be just possible at a little distance to suppose that a real lintel was there. And so on with other details. I have pointed out that such work is the inevitable result of employing ignorant contractors

* See appendix to my "Indian Craftsman."

and ignoring the traditional craftsmen; and that the only method of saving the traditional skill of Sinhalese craftsmen is to return to the old system of State recognition. If men in the future are to be able still to avail themselves of the spiritual and economic benefits of the union of art with labour characteristic of all true civilization in the past, the State must assume, as for example in thirteenth century Florence, the role of protector of the craftsmen, who must be supported, endowed, and respected no less than the other servants of the State, or of the church.

British influence has been adverse to Indian Art in other ways. The output of cheap and inferior carpets in jails went far to destroy the trade in well-made and fairly priced carpets, a fact so well-known as to need no further mention. Of the influence of art schools little need be said; by some the whole degeneration of Indian art has been attributed to them and while this is a great exaggeration, there can be no doubt that their influence has been pernicious. It is now otherwise in the case of certain art schools, particularly Lahore and Calcutta, but it is too late to arrest the harm already done, and still being done elsewhere. So also with the jails, there are many, such as Agra and Poona, where work of good quality is now done, and chemical dyes are totally avoided; but much of the evil is done, and the force of example is still seen in the case of such jails in Native States as continue to make use of chemical dyes, to the detriment of the quality of their productions (*e. g.*, Gwalior).

Indian kings have been great religious builders from the earliest times, spending their resources gladly on temples built to the glory of God, and hostels for the shelter of man. They were just such great builders as the earlier English kings. But now imagine the injury to English art that would have come about, if English independence had ceased in the time of Henry III, as a result of the rapacity of some nation of materialists and agnostics*—Westminster Abbey left unfinished, Gothic art no more the vehicle of the national religious sense; imagine the invaders also destroying the possibility of popular art in the other ways referred to, and you will have some picture of what has taken place in India.

But it is but fair to refer to the few efforts that have been made, directly or indirectly, by Englishmen, officially or otherwise, to save the Indian arts from extinction. We have occasional efforts to build in the style of the country, as in Lahore, but these are not more successful than XIXth century efforts in Europe to build in XIV century wise. We have the establishment of schools of art in India, with good intention, but, in the opinion of even most English artists, bad results; even where great and good work is done, as now in Calcutta, its continuance is at the mercy of chance selection of a Principal having knowledge and sympathy adequate to the situation. We have the publication of books and journals illustrating fine examples of Indian art; but these, valuable as they are, are really written by Englishmen for Englishmen, and are of more use to the English manufacturer than to the village craftsmen; and does the reproduction of details of architecture and jewellery (often ill-drawn by men not in the tradition) compensate in any way for the deserted workshops and forgotten knowledge of the hereditary craftsmen? Lord Curzon has done good service in securing the preservation of Indian monuments; but archæology is not art: and even his appeal to the Indian aristo-

* The relation between the British Government and Indian people is purely secular—a suggestion in itself of the evil necessarily resulting from the government of one nation by another, the difference of faith making impracticable that identification of sentiment between ruler and craftsmen which alone made possible such buildings as Westminster Abbey.

cracy at the Delhi exhibition seemed to them little more than the Englishman's strange fancy for Indian 'curiosities.' A certain Maharajah shortly after the utterance of that appeal had to entertain Lord Curzon; his own palace was a modern building, designed and furnished in a French style. To please the Viceroy he sent to Bombay for 20 lakhs worth of Bombay blackwood furniture, and put away the French stuff; but when Lord Curzon left, the latter all came out again! Now Bombay blackwood is but half Indian at best; but the Maharajah neither knew this, nor was actuated by any deeper motive than a desire to please the Viceroy. And so it must ever be, that the best meant endeavours of outsiders can effect but little; while a little germ of love for the motherland might effect everything. It is easier to destroy than to create; it is impossible for England to build up what she has demolished; if the re-awakening is to come at all, it will be the fruit of India's recognition of her national self; but that, alas, will be in spite of England's opposition, not with England's help! Not that all sympathetic and disinterested counsel is altogether thrown away; but that advice is a totally inadequate solution.

So much for external influence on Indian art; it has been on the whole an influence contributing to "the rapid deterioration that has of late befallen the great historical arts of India."* Let us for a time consider the changes in Indian society and ideas which have from within contributed to the same result.

* In charging England with the responsibility for much of the deterioration of Indian art, I do not forget that a world process of the same character is everywhere at work, and that England is only for us the particular medium through which these tendencies effect us. But "approved departmental methods, instead of reviving original creative activity, have done everything possible to suppress it, and, by rooting out the traditional practice, they have given a wholly unnecessary impulse to the natural process of decay which has acted upon all Eastern art in the last few generations" (E. B. Havell, the 'Studio' Vol. 44, p. 116). In the words of the group of artists already referred to (Morris, Crane, etc., 1879) "we cannot conceive that any thoughtful person will deny the responsibility of England in the matter, or the duty which a great country owes to the arts."

The internal influences are complex, and closely related to the external. Architecture is the mistress of all arts; and where architecture is neglected the lesser arts must also perish. Even Native States no longer give employment to the hereditary builders; and so blindly do individuals also imitate the examples of Europeans, that it is the echo of the English suburban villa which shapes the ideal of a house in the modern Indian mind. If England has in her public buildings set before us examples of bastard Anglo-Classic and Neo-Gothic architecture, we have made haste to blindly copy example. If Brussels carpets come from Europe, it is we who buy them in preference to the productions of Indian looms. If coloured crystal balls are made in England, it is we who buy them to 'adorn' our temples. If English dress appears unlovely and absurd on us, it is we ourselves who are responsible for the wearing of it. Nothing can possibly be more fatal to the arts than this attitude of snobbishness, or, at the best, weakness, which leads us to imitate without consideration. The Art of Life is now less and less for us ruled by principle, but more and more by impulse; and so it is natural that in our attitude towards art itself we are undisciplined and unprincipled. For this we are ourselves responsible; the fact of foreign rule need not compel the Indian to acquire a foreign mind; and as long as we so carelessly contribute ourselves to the decay of art amongst us, our complaint against others for the same thing loses force. Hope alone lies in the National ideal.

What has Swadeshi done for Indian art? Almost nothing; when a decaying industry can be used to political advantage it gives it loud support, and in this way the hand-loom industry of Bengal is receiving attention now; but the whole country from north to south is full of decaying industries and perishing hereditary skill, to save which no effort is made. Efforts are made to establish all sorts of factories for making soap, matches, cotton, nibs, biscuits and what not, while the men who can still weave, still build, still work in gold and silver, copper and wood and stone, are starving because their work is out of fashion. Swadeshi often ignores the things which India has from time immemorial made perfectly, to seek to manufacture things which it would be better to do without altogether, or to frankly buy from other nations more able to make them easily.

The Swadeshi impulse is as yet a too purely commercial one, too unimaginative, too solely based on an ideal of dull prosperity to greatly help the cause of Indian art. It is, indeed, rather art that can help Swadeshi, than Swadeshi, art. Things are bettering as the national consciousness develops; but those who now are benefited are the enterprising promoters of small capitalist concerns—not the traditional craftsmen. What cares the South Indian village weaver whether his Zemindar buys Manchester or Bombay cotton? What avails it for Indian culture if the mean design and glaring colours are printed in England or in India? Ought we not rather to starve than to compete with Europe on such degrading terms? Yet men must live; material necessities now more than ever control our lives; the day is far distant when work for an hour and a half will again suffice for daily bread-winning.* Men must live by manufacture, agriculture, or trade, or by the practice of some

* Some Swadeshi exhibits at the Calcutta exhibition of 1906 were so vulgar and stupid that, if it had been shown in an exhibition under European control, it could only have been done as a deliberate insult. Not without reason does Mr. Havell, in a most valuable article (Art, Ethics, and Economics in Hand-loom Weaving) appearing in 'East and West' for August, 1907, make the following statement, the truth of which cannot be disputed: "In India there has been during the last hundred years a continuous decline of public taste, so that at the present time the educated Indians probably stand behind the rest of the world in artistic understanding."

profession. But for all that, India is India still, and shall not even her material production be controlled by the spirit of her real self? If she is to grow wealthy, let it be by as far as possible ministering to the higher needs of men as in the past; let it be possible for the Swadeshist to buy Swadeshi manufactures because they are better, more beautiful or more enduring than the work of others. Let India supply the world again with beautiful fabrics, holding the market by sheer superiority of design and workmanship—a thing still possible if the existing traditional capacity of Indian craftsmen were rightly organized. There is a real demand in other lands for things worth making, things made well; if in England it still pays even a few groups of men to turn out linen, tapestry or carpets by hand, (for the sake of the fine quality of material, and still more for the art qualities of the accomplished work) it should still be possible for those who can work much cheaper, (and could still command the services of craftsmen possessing hereditary skill sufficient to make the fortune of any manufacturer in Europe) to find a market for their own best work. The aim must be for quality not quantity. There is no country in the world where so much capacity for design and workmanship exists; but we are recklessly flinging this, almost our greatest treasure, to the winds, and with it all spontaneous expression in art.

In the opinion of thinking men it must appear that it is not worth while being a nation at all, or making any attempt at political freedom, if India is to remain in the end thus enslaved at heart by purely material ideals. The national movement has no justification if it does not carry with it some hope of a new manifestation of the Indian genius in relation to the real things of life. The significance of the movement however consists just in this, that such a hope is indeed bound up with it.

I have spoken of *foreign* trade; but what is far more important, from the art point of view, is the *Indian* attitude towards Indian art. For Indian art can never be great, can never mean to Indians or foreigners what it once meant, until it is again made for Indians and can count upon their sympathy and comprehension as a birth-right. An art, which is primarily concerned with supplying the particular requirements of peoples entirely out of real touch with its producers, must always be slavish and artificial. It is as evil a thing* for us to supply the American market with bales of cheap and vulgar phulkaris† embroidered in offensive colours and mean designs and sloppy needlework, as it is for Manchester to send us bicycle-patterned saris. The only true remedies that can be effectual are the re-generation of Indian taste, and the re-establishment of some standard of quality. Nearly thirty years ago Sir George Birdwood said truly that—

> "Indian native gentlemen and ladies should make it a point of culture never to wear any clothing or ornaments but of native manufacture and strictly native design, constantly purified by comparison with the best examples and the models furnished by the sculptors of Amaravati, Sanchi and Barhut".

Indian art can only revive and flourish if it is beloved by Indians themselves.

Somewhat apart from architecture stands the question of Western influence on Indian painting. This influence has been exerted very largely through the schools of art. In these schools there is done much oil and water colour painting, some of it clever, some extremely poor, but all quite undistinguishable—unless by general weakness of drawing—from

* If anyone should doubt that the attempts to wrest the Indian market in textiles from the hands of the village printer and dyer has had any but a grossly degrading effect on the English manufacture and English workman, let him study the specimen of English prints reproduced in the Journal of Indian Art, Vol. VII, as examples for comparison with Indian work. For the converse result, see Vol. II, p. 27, of the same Journal, exhibiting degenerate Indian embroidery.

† See Mrs. Steel, Journal of Indian Art, Vol. 2, 1888.

ordinary European work of the same class. The best known exponent of this style, though not I believe a school of art pupil, has been the oil-painter Ravi Varma, whose works, constantly reproduced, are everywhere popular in India. The 'educated' public of modern India, having learnt to judge all things by what was understood to be a Western standard, misunderstood the conventional art of India herself; sincere and tender, it was often over-formal, and represented in many cases the decline rather than the zenith of tradition; and so the public, seeking for an art easily understood without preparation or effort, welcomed this painter who broke through traditions and gave them realistic and sentimental pictures of familiar subjects.

A picture of 'Sita in Exile' well illustrates the difference between Tagore's and Ravi Varma's work. In the latter's 'Sita in the Asoka Grove' we see only a woman bullied by her captor; in the Sita by Tagore we see the embodiment of a national ideal. In Ravi Varma's well-known picture of Sarasvati, again, the lotus-seat—essentially an abstract symbol of divine and other—worldly origin, is represented as a real flower growing in a lake; so that the spectator is led immediately away from the ideal, to wonder how the stalk can be strong enough to support a full-grown woman. I say 'woman' advisedly, because Ravi Varma's divinities, in spite of their many arms, are very human, and often not very noble human types. At best the goddesses are 'pretty': stronger condemnation of what should be ideal religious art it would be hard to find.

It has indeed been Ravi Varma's reward for choosing Indian subjects, that he has been to some degree a true nationalising influence; but had he been also a true artist with the gift of great imagination, this influence must have been tenfold deeper and greater. He is the landmark of a great opportunity, not perhaps wholly missed, but ill availed of. Theatrical conceptions, want of imagination, want of restraint, anecdotal aims and a lack of Indian feeling in the treatment of sacred and epic subjects are his faults. His art is not truly national—he merely plays with local colour. His gods and heroes are men cast in a very common mould, who find themselves in situations for which they lack a proper dignity. Ravi Varma's pictures, in a word, are not national art; they are such as any European student could paint, after only a superficial study of Indian life and literature.

A reaction from these ideals is represented by what has been called the New School of Indian Painting, founded by Abanindra Nath Tagore, Vice-Principal of the Calcutta School of Art. In Mr. Havell, late Principal of this School, India for the first time found a European artist able to divest himself of early prejudices and willing as well to learn as to teach. In the 'Studio' of July, 1908, Mr. Havell relates how when he went to the Calcutta School twelve years ago, it was like other schools, an institution established by a benevolent Government for the purpose of revealing to Indians the superiority of European art. Mr. Havell succeeded in revising the whole course of instruction, making Indian art the basis of the teaching. This was not done without opposition from the Bengalis themselves, who saw in these proceedings only a sinister attempt to discourage 'high art' in Bengal. Two pieces of good fortune attended Mr Havell's efforts, one the opportunity of acquiring for the Calcutta gallery a large number of paintings of the finest Moghal period, many of them by Shah Jahan's court painters, and secondly, and most important, the discovery of Mr. Abanindra Nath Tagore. This artist had until then followed European ideas of artistic expression, but soon realised the significance of Indian art traditions and set himself to study their technique and recover something of their spirit. Mr. Tagore afterwards became Vice-Principal, and finally acting Principal of the Calcutta School of art,—the first, and with the exception of Lahore, and now, perhaps, of Madras, the only modern school of art in India related effectively to the past traditions of Indian art, and to the new national spirit of self-realisation. Tagore's own work is a significant omen of what may be given to the world of India, when the Indian people realize to the full the duty which is theirs, not to borrow what they can from others, but themselves to give.

Of Tagore's work, a number of examples have been reproduced in the 'Studio,' and others in the 'Modern Review'. The best of them is perhaps 'The Banished Yaksha', illustrating the well-known work of Kālidāsa, the Megha Duta. Mr. Tagore has painted also 'The Passing of Shah Jahan'; the 'Siddhas of the Upper Air'; 'Aurangzib Examining the Head of Dāra' and there are other important works, some of which are reproduced in Mr. Havell's 'Indian Painting and Sculpture'. There can be traced in these works both European and Japanese influence; but their significance lies in what is after all their essential Indianness. These delicate water colours, portfolio pictures like those that delighted the Mughal Emperor's courts of old, are supremely tender, and carry in them that mingled reticence and revelation that belong to all great art, but which demand something also of the public, before they can be fully understood and realised. Such work, a true expression of Indian nationalism, is the flowering of the old tradition; a flower that speaks not only of past loveliness, but is strong and vigorous with promise of abundant fruit.

Two pupils have indeed already followed in Tagore's footsteps. The pictures, 'The Flight of Lakshman Sen', by Surendra Nath Ganguly, and 'Raja Vikram and the Vampire', by Nanda Lal

Bose, reproduced in the 'Studio' of July, 1908, are full of promise; and indeed remarkable as the work of men so young. The best of Nanda Lal Bose's work is the wonderful 'Sati' reproduced by Mr. Havell. Almost equally perfect in another way is the 'Kaikeyi,' of which a number of copies have been reproduced in Japan for the Indian Society of Oriental Art.

Great art or science is the flower of a free national life pouring its abundant energy into ever new channels, giving some new intimation of a truth and harmony before unknown or forgotten. It is not strange that India, after a thousand years of alien government, often puritan and now philistine, economically and morally impoverished, should have lost her position in the world of art. But we believe that India stands upon the threshold of a freedom and a unity greater than any yet realised. If this be so, we need not fear for Indian art; for the new life must find its self-expression. It rests with each individual to make this fruition possible.

Art of the East and of the West.*

CHAPTER VII.

IT is not possible to understand the art of India without some comprehension of the whole culture and historical tradition of which it is an immediate expression. It is impossible to treat of art as an isolated phenomenon apart from the spiritual and physical life of the people who gave it birth. Indian art cannot be understood by those without sympathy for Indian culture; and this is still a rare thing. The orthodox Christian, the materialist, and the Imperialist are all, in so far as they are what these names imply, constitutionally unable to sympathise with the ideals of Indian civilisation. Indian art is essentially religious; and those who are entirely ignorant of and hopelessly out of sympathy with Indian religions, as well as those who in the name of Puritanism would secularise or abolish art entirely, have not in them a capacity for understanding. Even with the best intentions, the study of Indian art proves difficult. There have until lately been no books to guide the student and no collections of Indian painting and sculpture, except those brought together with a purely archaeological purpose. Unfamiliarity with Indian religious philosophy, and its traditional expression in art and literature, and the now complete divorce between art and life in Europe, have added to the difficulties of those who have sought to know

* This article originally formed part of a lecture given to the members of the Art-workers' guild, and is primarily phrased as if for European readers.

anything of Indian art. A majority—from Ruskin onwards—have rested happy in the conviction that there was nothing to be known.

I give a typical example of the ordinary attitude, a quotation from Mr. Maskell's book on "Ivories":

"There is a sameness, a repetition, an overloading, a crowding and elaboration of detail which become wearisome before we have gone very far. We are spoken to of things, and in a language of which we are ignorant. We regard them with a listless kind of attention. In a word, we are not interested. We feel that the artist has ever been bound and enslaved by the traditions of Hindoo mythology. We are met at every turn by the interminable processions of monstrous gods and goddesses, these Buddhas and Krishnas, Vishnus and Ramas, these hideous deities with animals' heads and innumerable arms, these dancing women with expressionless faces and strange garments. . . . . In his figures the Hindoo artist seems absolutely incapable—it may be reluctant—to reproduce the human form; he ignores anatomy, he appears to have no idea of giving any expression to the features. There is no distinction between the work of one man and another. Is the name of a single artist familiar? The reproduction of type is literal: one divinity resembles another, and we can only distinguish them by their attributes, or by the more or less hideous occupations in which they may be supposed to be engaged."

This ignorant and childish rhodomontade is here quoted only because it is so typical. Perhaps the easiest way to show its true value would be to ask you to imagine similar words spoken by an Oriental, who should substitute the word "Christian" for the word "Hindu": "Enslaved by the traditions of Christian mythology, interminable processions of crucifixes and Madonnas"—would not this be an idle criticism of mediaeval European art?

I take another instance. Professor Nelson Fraser, an English teacher in India, and a student of Indian art and religious ideas, tells us that one day he had a young lady visitor from England, something of an artist, and she was examining his treasures gathered from East and West and of all periods. She flitted lightly over the Hindu bronzes and settled down on a case of Greek coins. He remonstrated against this, and pointed out that she might see the Greek coins any day at the British Museum, whereas she might never see the bronzes again at all. "I don't care for grotesques," she answered; "I don't understand these things."

A characteristic difference between Eastern and Western art is found in the sacred images. In Western art, the sacred images are almost always entirely human in form, in Eastern art they are sometimes four-handed, sometimes zoomorphic, sometimes grotesque. In part this represents in the West, the lasting influence of Hellenism with its representations of the beautiful Olympians as perfect men; and is due to the Western temperament which more naturally than the Eastern seeks for the realisation of objective perfection. In the East it represents the fact that Eastern art traditions carry an inheritance from Egypt and Assyria, and that common 'Early Asiatic' behind all Eastern art, inheritances that a brief period of classic influence failed to affect to any significant extent. But this distinction of images is not essentially due to art, but rather to the centre of gravity of religious ideas; and yet even here the line of division between East and West is not so sharp as it appears. The images of the West have been almost entirely those of the incarnation, an *avatār*, or of saints; these of course, just as an image of Rāma or Sītā would be, are altogether human in form; but when the Western artist has to represent an immanent divinity, the Holy Ghost, at once he falls back upon an animal symbol,—the dove. To the true mystic it is evident that a representation of the divine in human form carries with it a certain limitation—it is not easy to constantly recall that the anthropomorphic appearance is but an appearance, a manifestation of the deity, and not the deity himself. And the anthropomorphic image easily degenerates, as the form of Eros degenerated into a Cupid, and Nikē became a woman stooping to tie her sandal, as the Virgin and Child of Early Italian art became at a later period the pretty domestic picture of the artist's wife and child. Indian religion has been always a search for the infinite, seeking to escape the limitations of individuality and time and space; how could it then be satisfied with the beautiful divine humanities of Hellas, or with representations of merely human figures? We must then in looking at Oriental art judge, not by our own preconceived ideas, but by its own standards. If we cannot sympathise with the aims of an alien art, so be it, it is our limitation. It may be thus a limitation in some that they cannot realise in full all the significance of the art of Hellas; it is a limitation imposed by temperament and inheritance. But they recognize the futility of judging it by an Indian standard, because the Greek artist did not even want to say what the Indian strove to say. It is equally futile to criticise Indian art by a Hellenic standard. Even in limitations there are advantages; through concentration comes understanding, intensity, and fruitfulness, while eclecticism brings with it the danger of indifference. But limitations need not mean intolerance: and as it is worth while for man and woman to try to understand each other, however far their points of view must also differ, so also it is worth while for the East and West to understand each other's art. Perhaps in their difference humanity will find a complementary perfection greater than any single manifestation of the human spirit can achieve alone. If then humanity would be so much poorer for the loss of either art, do we do well to complain of either for being what it has never striven to be, do we do wisely in rejecting an alien art contemptuously because it does not recognize the standards that have moulded our own?

There are indeed many difficulties in the way of the Western student of Indian art, but they are not insuperable. The first perhaps lies in the fact that the Indian ideal of beauty is not altogether the same as the Greek ideal which has influenced all Western art; and a greater difficulty lies perhaps in the fact that for India, art, to be great, need not necessarily be beautiful at all, unless we give to 'beauty,' the deeper meaning of 'harmony,' which really belongs to it. In India the beautiful and the grotesque are not distinguished as the greater and lesser kinds of art; each manifests its own idea, each may be a harmony. There is something in great ideal art that transcends the limited conceptions of beauty and ugliness and makes any criticism founded on such a basis seem but idle words.

In art, as in life, we pray for deliverance from the bondage of the pairs of opposites, the "Delusion of the Pairs."

And even when the representation of physical human beauty is the immediate aim, we find that the ideal of the human form is different in East and West. The robust muscularity and activity of the Greek athletic statue, or of Michael Angelo's ideal, is repugnant to the lover of the repose, and the smooth and slender refinement of the bodies and limbs of Orientals. It is the same with the features and the colour. For example, the perfect colour in our eyes, which we call fair, is a light golden brown, and not at all the snow-white paleness of the European ideal. But the real division lies deeper still. The absence of mystery, the altogether limited ideal of Greek art, its satisfaction with the expression of merely physical beauty, conceived as an end in itself; the dead mechanical perfection of its decorative details; the intellectual rather than imaginative aims—all these things make it possible for us to look upon the great classic art which has so profoundly influenced the aims of later Western art, as having striven for, and perhaps attained, a goal to which we do not ourselves aspire. In these remarks I refer to Pheidian and later art only, not to such beautiful archaic art as the Antenor of the Acropolis.

"Greek work as known to us," says Prof. Gardner, "is restrained on the emotional side; nor has it any touch of mysticism." In most Pheidian Greek art there is little or nothing that corresponds to such work as the "Bacchae" of Euripides in literature. The Venus of Milo, for example, is only a very beautiful figure, a combination of perfections, intellectually selected and skilfully combined. It is limited by the idea of external, physical and human beauty. This is perhaps an indication of the point at which the Eastern and Western views of art part company. The Western artist sees nature with his eyes and judges art by intellectual and aesthetic standards. The Indian seeks truth in his inner consciousness, and judges of its expression by metaphysical and imaginative standards. Art for him is not to please, but to manifest.

We are told that Zeuxis, when commissioned to paint a figure of Helen for the people of Croton, stipulated to be allowed to use as models five of the most beautiful virgins of the city. The Indian artist, on the other hand, would have demanded opportunity for meditation and mental concentration, in order that he might visualise the idea of Helen in his inner consciousness, aiming rather at discovery than creation, desiring rather to draw back the veil from the face of superwoman than to combine visible perfections by a process of intellectual selection. The result would be a work suggesting, more or less perfectly in accordance with his keenness of inner vision and technical capacity for its material embodiment, the real Helen as she lived in the national consciousness, a Helen more real than she who in the flesh brought death and sorrow to the Greek and Trojan heroes.

The Greek, indeed, was above the "aesthetic nihilism" (to borrow a phrase from Professor Gardner) which sees the aim of art in the faithful reproduction of nature; but he made an intellectual selection from natural forms, instead of seeking the highest truth where alone it is to be found, in one's inner consciousness. It is true that Greek art was to an extent religious; but it failed in the greatest qualities because the religion expressed in it was in no sense transcendental, and this is the explanation of the humanism, almost the *bourgeois* character, one might say, of the Greek gods. There are, for instance, many Apollos, of which it is said that there are equally good grounds for regarding them as representations, or even portraits, of athletes.*

Hinduism, like Christianity, knew that life could not be an end in itself, but that the true end of our existence transcends it. But the Greeks and Romans placed this end absolutely in life itself. This limitation could not fail to find expression as much in their art as their religion. "The Greeks" says Burne Jones, "give you the godlike beauty, strength, majesty. They suggest that wisdom is Godlike. They nowhere suggest the mystery of life."†

In all these respects Greek literature is immeasurably greater than Greek art. It is unfortunate that almost all Greek art belongs to the Olympian, not to the mystic, side of Greek religion.

The great cat-gods of Egypt, the sublime Buddhas of Java, the four-handed gods of India, even the great Chinese dragon, are greater imaginative art, belong more to the divine in man, than do the Hermes of Praxiteles or the Venus of Milo. The ideal of the last is limited, and the very fact and possibility of its attainment show it. I do not mean, of course, that even post-Pheidian Greek art could be spared from the world, or that it is not one of

* Walters, "The Art of the Greeks" (p. 73).
† E. B. J. Life (p. 263).

the great achievements of humanity; only that it was in certain respects definitely limited, and does not necessarily stand on a pinnacle by itself as the greatest of all art the world has seen. Once the spell of this limited ideal is broken, you can never again be satisfied by it, but seek in art for that which has often been suggested but never can, and never will, be perfectly expressed—the portrayal not merely of perfect men, but of perfect and entire divinity. You seek for an art which, however imperfectly, seeks to represent neither particular things nor merely physical or human grandeur, but which aims at an intimation of the universe, and that universe conceived not as an empirical phenomenon, but as noumenon within yourself.

And if it is thus possible for India to feel unsatisfied with even the refined, and in some degree idealistic art of Greece, it will be clear how much less the naturalism and aestheticism of modern European art appeals to her—the pictures of Poynter, the portraits of Sargent, the landscapes on the exhibition walls, the jewellery of Lalique, or to go farther back, the wood-carving of Grinling Gibbons or the naturalistic borders of the later mediaeval manuscripts. All these are pictorial, reminiscent, or anecdotal in their character. But when we come back to the thirteenth and fourteenth centuries, with the glorious work of the imagers at Chartres, the sweet ivory Madonnas, the crisp and prickly borders of the manuscripts, and the Gothic rose bequeathed to later times as the symbol of the idealism of the Middle Ages, then at last we find an art that expresses or endeavours to express something of that which we too desire to say. Nothing is more remarkable than the "Gothicness" and, in Ruskin's sense, the "Christianity" of Oriental art. From this point of view, indeed, I should like to classify Gothic, Egyptian, Indian, and Chinese art as Christian, and Greek, Roman, Renaissance, and modern European as pagan, or to use more general terms, as religious and materialistic respectively.

To speak again of the present day: it is not that there is no art in the West which, from the Indian point of view, is great; there has been such art; but it has come only from men fighting desperately against the spirit of the age, living in another world of theirs and ours. Of these, Burne-Jones and William Morris are the greatest: the former in that his work possesses something of that impersonality and aloofness which we seek for, and because he uses form less for its own sake than as a manifestation of something more changeless and eternal; because, too, he was made wise by love to paint not the beauty of the passing hour or the transient emotion, but the changeless might and glory of the gods and heroes; and Morris was great because he proved again that all art is one, the distinction between art and craft illusory, and that this single art is not merely a trivial pastime, but essential to humanity and civilisation.

In the immediate future we may, both in England and in India, have less and less art. English art flourishes at present mainly as an exotic, a luxury for those who can afford it. It appeals to a special class, and is not a spontaneous expression of the national life as a whole. Its appeal, like that of much of the later Japanese art which finds acceptance in the West, is trivial, not fundamental; it must be pretty and pleasing; its aim is primarily aesthetic, where it should be prophetic. This divergence between art and life and art and religion is increasing. It is a sign of the times. I cannot think it possible for great art to flourish again in England, or in India, till we have all once more civilised ourselves, and learnt to believe in something more real and more eternal than the external face of nature—until we are able to re-unite art with labour, and imagination with technique.

The Influence of Greek on Indian Art.

CHAPTER VIII.

THE orthodox archaeological view of the history of Indian sculpture is much as follows:—

The Early Indian School (B.C. 250—A.D. 50) is a compound of Hellenistic, Persian and Indian elements. From this period we have scarcely any detached statues in stone, and no representations of Buddha, whether free or in low relief. Of the greatest importance is the second or Kushān Period (A.D. 50—350), to which the two local schools of Gandhāra and Amarāvati belong. The works of the Gandhāra school are "probably equal in merit to much of the contemporary sculpture in the provinces of the Roman empire" and are "infinitely superior to any truly Indian production." Images of Buddha become abundant; the representations of Buddha and personages of Buddhist mythology are adaptations of Greek gods; "the ideal type of Buddha. . . . was created for Buddhist art by foreigners." The type thus evolved was the foundation of all later representations of Buddha. The classic influence is traceable in all later work, and responsible for most of the little value it possesses. "After 300 A.D. Indian sculpture properly so called hardly deserves to be reckoned as art. The figures both of men and animals become stiff and formal, and the idea of power is clumsily expressed by the multiplication of members. The many-headed, many-armed gods and goddesses whose images crowd the walls and roofs of mediaeval temples have no pretensions to beauty, and are frequently hideous and grotesque. . . . . Every mediaeval temple of importance throughout India might be cited as illustrating these remarks;" individual examples merit consideration only as "marking stages in the decadence of Indian art."*

Those who do hold other views disagree, not as to the fact of the Greek-Roman influence in the Gandhāra period, but as to its ultimate importance in the history of Oriental art; and form a very different estimate of the value of Indian sculpture after 300 A.D. So far from foreigners having given to India the ideal type of Buddha, the Gandhāra sculptures should perhaps be regarded as the work of late Greek-Roman craftsmen striving in vain to interpret Indian ideals. The sculptures themselves, crowded and effeminate, show how little of value in art the Western world at this time had to offer to the East. Foreign influence on Indian art, during the first few centuries of the Christian era, was perhaps as much to be regretted as the results of Western influence on Indian art at the present day. Had Asiatic art developed independently of late classic influence, it might at an earlier period have freed itself from various disadvantageous conditions. As a matter of fact, it was not until the direct effects of the foreign influence were passing away, that the Indian ideal emerged, and the truly Indian schools of sculpture rose. What has been most of all misunderstood by archaeologists is the nature of this influence. They have confused the assimilation of foreign forms and foreign technique with artistic inspiration. No sooner is the same art studied by artists, as in the case of Mr. Havell's work on 'Indian Sculpture and Painting,' or of Mr. Laurence Binyon's on 'Painting in the Far East,' than it is discovered that the archaeologists may be correct

V. A. Smith, Imperial Gazetteer of India, II, Ch. III.
A. Grunwedel, Buddhist Art in India, p. 68.

as to outward details, but entirely misled as to informing spirit.

It is probable that none of the most beautiful or important Indian sculpture can be certainly assigned to a date *earlier* than 300 A.D. The true problem of Indian art-criticism is the study of the development of the Indian ideal, and its gradual emancipation from the fetters of borrowed art formulas little adapted to its adequate expression. This development and emancipation went on during the centuries when Hinduism itself was emerging from earlier Brahmanism and Buddhism, when Vishnu and Siva took final shape in the Indian imagination, that is to say, as far as it is possible to lay down a date between the third and eighth centuries of the Christian era. When the philosophy of Indian art is understood, it will be seen how little it could have depended upon the art philosophy even of classic Greece, and the idea of tracing its inspiration to late Greek-Roman influence will appear still more absurd. The philosophies of Greek and of Indian art are poles apart. Putting aside the rare and beautiful fragments of archaic art, and vase paintings that illustrate the mystic and orgiastic sides of Greek religion, Greek art has in it no touch of mysticism; the Greek representations of the gods belong entirely to the Olympian aspect of Greek religion. They are but grand and beautiful men; sometimes, as in the case of many Apollos, it is uncertain even whether the representation is of a god or of an athlete.* Indian art on the contrary is essentially transcendental; its concern is not with the representation of perfect men, but with the intimation of an unknown Divinity, the symbolism of the Infinite. It has, though to a less degree, I think, than the art of Egypt, that sense of 'Being beyond (or behind)

* Quoted on p. 88.

Appearance' which we miss in the Greek representations of beautiful Olympians.

And so we may read anew the meaning of the Gandhāra sculptures, and see in them, not the influence of Greek-Roman art on Indian art, but the influence of Indian art upon Greek-Roman. We see, not foreign craftsmen creating an ideal afterwards imitated throughout the East, but we see the transforming influence of Indian philosophy, at the time when Hinduism in its modern aspects was emerging from a diversity of origins, exerted upon, and gradually Indianising, Greek-Roman art. The foreign influence coincided with the first general development of ritual and imagery; but the late classic gods of Europe were ill fitted to express the infinities of Indian thought. And so we gradually find in the later Gandhāra work the germ of the Indian ideal,—centred at first round the image of Buddha conceived as a divine being, with a spiritual, superhuman body—and soon finding expression in a thousand forms of gods and angels. By the eighth or ninth century this truly Indian art had reached its zenith; the artistic canons of Sukrācārya and others had already been formulated, the necessity of meditation and visualisation perfectly realised, and the finest work of Elephanta and Borobodur was done. The Mahāyāna Buddhist bronzes of Ceylon and Java attained the highest level of attainment in the seventh or eighth century. Hindu art flourished still for several centuries. The advent of the Muhammadans then put an end to the natural development of Hindu art in the north, but work of the finest type, and perhaps the most distinctively Indian of all, continued to be produced in Southern India and in Nepal for some centuries.

At last the great traditions seemed to lose their strength; the guilds of artists little by little lost their power and culture, and at the same time the corrupting influence of Europe

PLATE VI.

THE POET SADI LISTENING TO A SINGER.

was felt, until at the present day neither the old traditions, nor any new development, except in special cases, reveal the real artistic instinct of the Indian people. Such, from the Indian point of view, is a brief reading of the history of Hindu art. That history in all its detail remains yêt to be written; the day is far distant when we can date a bronze or a stone sculpture with certainty even to a century, lacking the evidence of inscriptions; but when the history of Indian art is thus at last made known, and correlated with the life and ideas of the people, it will be abundantly clear how small was the ultimate importance of the Classic influence in the development of all that is most essential in it. Indeed, if originality be regarded as of so much importance, it is certain that no art in the world is further removed in aims and in form from that of Greece, than is the art of the Dravidian South, or even the Buddhist art of Borobodur. And it must always be borne in mind that if a survival of Greek influence is anywhere traceable in later Indian art, this no more itself invalidates a claim for genius and originality in that art, than the fact that all his plots are borrowed makes Shakespeare a poor dramatist. No mature art stands absolutely alone, or lacks an inheritance from other arts. It is the nature and extent of this inheritance in Indian art, which have been misunderstood and exaggerated. The question, moreover, is one at issue essentially between archaeologists and artists who accept their facts but question their interpretation; it is not a question between patriots claiming originality—obvious in any case—and foreign students denying it. Compared with the vital significance of Indian art as a manifestation of the Indian genius, the question is, indeed, of hardly more than academic importance.

Education in India.

CHAPTER IX.

ONE of the most remarkable features of British rule in India has been the fact that the greatest injuries done to the people of India have taken the outward form of blessings. Of this, Education is a striking example; for no more crushing blows have ever been struck at the roots of Indian National evolution than those which have been struck, often with other, and the best intentions, in the name of Education. It is sometimes said by friends of India that the National movement is the natural result of English education, and one of which England should in truth be proud, as showing that, under 'civilisation' and the Pax Britannica, Indians are becoming, at last, capable of self-government. The facts are otherwise. If Indians are still capable of self-government, it is in spite of all the anti-national tendencies of a system of education that has ignored or despised almost every ideal informing the national culture.

By their fruits ye shall know them. The most crushing indictment of this Education is the fact that it destroys, in the great majority of those upon whom it is inflicted, all capacity for the appreciation of Indian culture. Speak to the ordinary graduate of an Indian University, or a student from Ceylon, of the ideals of the Mahābhārata—he will hasten to display his knowledge of Shakespeare; talk to him of religious philosophy—you find that he is an atheist of the crude type common in Europe a generation ago, and that not only has he no religion, but he is as lacking in philosophy as the average Englishman; talk to him of Indian music—he will produce a gramophone or a harmonium, and inflict upon you one or both; talk to him of Indian dress or jewellery—he will tell you that they are uncivilised and barbaric; talk to him of Indian art—it is news to him that such a thing exists; ask him to translate for you a letter written in his own mother-tongue—he does not know it.* He is indeed a stranger in his own land.

Yes, English educators of India, you do well to scorn the Babu graduate; he is your own special production, made in your own image; he might be one of your very selves. Do you not recognize the likeness? Probably you do not; for you are still hidebound in that impervious skin of self-satisfaction that enabled your most pompous and self-important philistine, Lord Macaulay, to believe that a single shelf of a good European library was worth all the literature of India, Arabia, and Persia. Beware lest in a hundred years the judgment be reversed, in the sense that Oriental culture will occupy a place even in European estimation, ranking at least equally with Classic. Meanwhile you have done well-nigh all that could be done to eradicate it in the land of its birth.

England, suddenly smitten with the great idea of 'civilising' India, conceived that the way to do this, was to make Indians like Englishmen. To this task England set herself with the best will in the world, not at all realising that, as has been so well said by the Abbé Dubois:

> "To make a new race of the Hindus, one would have to begin by undermining the very foundations of their civilisation, religion and polity, and by turning them into atheists and barbarians."

* I describe the extreme product of English education, as seen for example in Ceylon. Not all of these statements apply equally to every part of India. The remarks on dress and music are of universal application.

H

And no words of mine could better describe the typical product of Macaulayism. Even suppose success were possible, and educated Indians were to acquire in some numbers, a thoroughly English point of view: this in itself would be damning evidence of failure, not merely because the English point of view is already sufficiently disseminated in a world of growing monotony, or even because of its many and serious limitations, but because it would prove that the education had failed to educate, that is, to *draw out* or set free the characteristic qualities of the taught. And in actual fact, it is not the English point of view that is acquired, but a caricature of it.

Imagine an ordinary English schoolmaster set down to educate the youth of Classic Greece. Obviously he could teach the Greek innumerable facts; but it is difficult to see how he could have taken any adequate part in his serious education. Merely to inform is not to educate; and into how little of the inner life of Greece, its religion and ideals, could the English schoolmaster, for all his Classic education, truly enter. The English schoolmaster to-day knows less of Indian culture and sympathises far less with Indian ideals, than he could with those of Greece. You cannot educate by ignoring (being ignorant of) the ideals of the taught, and setting up an ideal which they do not at heart acknowledge; if at the same time considerations of material advantage secure an outward acceptance, perhaps, even a willing acceptance, of the alien formula, the destruction of indigenous culture is assured.

All departments of education in India—primary, secondary and university—are directly or indirectly controlled by Government. A few indigenous institutions for imparting a knowledge of Sanskrit and Arabic carry on a forlorn struggle for existence. A few modern institutions, such as the Central Hindu

College in Benares, and the Hardwar Gurukula, are carried on entirely without Government aid; but most of these are bound to the University curriculum, as otherwise their students would be unable to obtain degrees. Two-thirds of Indian Arts Colleges are Missionary Institutions,—equally bound to the Government codes and selected text-books. The net result is that Indian culture is practically ignored in modern education; for Indian culture, whether Hindu or Muhammadan, is essentially religious, and so, regardless of the example of almost every Indian ruler since history began, the Government practises toleration—by ignoring Indian culture,—and the Missionary practises intolerance—by endeavouring to destroy that culture, in schools where education is offered as a bribe, and where the religion of the people is of set purpose undermined. The great tragedy of the present situation lies in this, that the schools are not part of Indian life (as were the *tols* and *maktabs* of the past), but antagonistic to it. Of the two types of English schools in India, Government and Missionary, the one ignores, the other endeavours to break down the ideals of the home. Sir George Birdwood truly says: "Our education has destroyed their love of their own literature, the quickening soul of a people, and their delight in their own arts and, worst of all, their repose in their own traditional and national religion. It has disgusted them with their own homes—their parents, their sisters, their very wives. It has brought discontent into every family so far as its baneful influences have reached."

The real difficulty at the root of all questions of Indian education is this, that modern 'education,' this education which Englishmen are so proud of having 'given' to India, is really based on the general assumption—nearly universal in England—that India is a *savage* country, which it is England's divine mission to *civilize*. This is the more or less

H 2

conscious underlying principle throughout. The facts were more truly realised by Sir Thomas Munro, when he wrote that "if civilisation were to be made an article of commerce between the two countries, England would soon be heavily in debt."

None can be true educators of the Indian people who do not inherit their traditions, or cannot easily work in a spirit of perfect reverence for those traditions. Others can be, not educators, but merely teachers of particular subjects. As such there is still room in India for English teachers; but they should be, not in power, but subordinate; they should be engaged by, paid by, and responsible to Indian managers, as, in Japan, English teachers are responsible to Japanese authorities. Professor Nelson Fraser, in a valuable discussion upon "The English Teacher in India," * shows how little the English teacher can know of the real life of the Indian people, and deduces that --

> "The Englishman is the last person to put forward any view as to possible reforms in Hindu institutions."

To do so, should not, indeed, be conceived as part of the English teacher's function—a fact which most English teachers (other than missionaries) are in the end driven reluctantly to admit. At first it is otherwise.

> "The conscientious professor does not merely desire to impart knowledge, but to impart useful knowledge, which will elevate the lives of his pupils; and he may perhaps wish to help them to apply it. Is there any prospect of his assisting this task? I suppose many teachers come to India with the hope of doing so; I should like to ask each of them, in the hour of his final departure, when he gave it up, and why. Possibly he would answer, when he candidly admitted to himself the impossibility of knowing much about India."

For the English Professor is debarred by ignorance of the language (very rarely adequately overcome), and by exclusion from familiarity with

* 'Indian Review,' April 1907.

the home life of Indians, from ever really understanding them.

The English Professor who arrives in India at the age, let us say, of twenty-five, is generally qualified to teach one or more special subjects, such as Chemistry, English Literature, or Greek. Ten years of sympathetic study of Indian religious philosophy, Sanskrit or Pali, some vernacular language, Indian history,* art, music, literature and etiquette might enable him to understand the problem of Indian education, probably would do so, prejudice apart; but the more he thus understood, the less would he wish to interfere, for he would either be Indianised at heart, or would have long realised the hopeless divergence between his own and Indian ideals; he would have learnt that true reforms come only from within, and slowly. But English teachers have neither the time nor the inclination to spend ten years, or even two, in such a study of Indian culture; and so, when, as often happens, they rise to a position of power, the Fellowship of some University, the Headship of a College, or even of a Department of Public Instruction, they cheerfully apply the solutions suited (or unsuited, as the case may be) to an English environment, to problems the elementary and fundamental conditions of which they do not understand, nor through mere book-learning can ever come to understand.

It must be understood that 'change' and (real) 'progress' are not interchangeable terms. The idea of education must be separated from the notion of altering the structure of Indian society,—still one of the avowed objects of the Western educator. As we have seen, though it may require alteration, and certainly cannot remain unchanged, or be

* Not merely recent history, but especially the periods in which the ideals of Indian civilisation were partly realised—Asoka, the Guptas, Akbar.

restored in any old form, yet the English teacher is of all men essentially ill-qualified to contribute to the solution of the problem. Even Sir Henry Craik, however, who thinks that English education in India is in its main lines "hopelessly wrong," and says that it is the opinion of every man capable of judging that it requires recasting, goes on to speak of the "hopeless hindrances" which it is necessary "to contend against." "The system of caste," he says, "the habits of the people, their inertness in manual labour, their fixed idea that clerical work has a dignity of its own—all these will take long before they are overcome."

What an incredible relief it would be to all concerned if the 'educator' would for a little while give over his 'contending,' and concern himself with education. For education, and the destruction of caste, purdah and religion are not convertible terms; education is the building up of character, essentially a constructive, not a contentious, process. Too often the "contention" is a tilting at a windmill; or the educator himself may be the *fons et origo* of the evil to be remedied. Take the last point raised by Sir Henry Craik, the idea of the dignity of clerical work. This is no more than a natural development resulting from the type of education offered, and the example set, by Englishmen. They with pain and labour have destroyed and are still endeavouring to destroy the caste idea of the dignity and duty of the heaven-ordained work, whether clerical or manual, to which a man is born; they in their educational system have ignored the Indian Gospel, wherein a well-known text declares, "Better is one's own duty, albeit insignificant, than even the well-executed duty of another." It is childish to be surprised at the result of a deliberate policy.

However convinced the English or Anglicised Indian educator may be of the superior value of

European ideals, he must even then as an educator realise that you can only educate by means of ideals accepted by the taught. Ideals are not to be transferred from one people to another as easily as furniture from house to house. It is only too easy to ridicule and to disparage, but when you have destroyed belief in one ideal it is not easy to secure acceptance of another. Not only, then, are the ideals of Indian civilization actually higher than those of any other, at least in our view; but, were it not so, it would still be true that only by means of those ideals can the Indian people be educated.

The aim of education in India must be no longer the cultivation of the English point of view or an ability to use the English formula correctly. In the words of Sir Henry Craik, it is necessary to abandon

> "the senseless attempt to turn an Oriental into a bad imitation of a Western mind. . . . . . . It is not a triumph for our education—it is, on the contrary a satire upon it—when we find the sons of leading natives expressly discouraged by their parents from acquiring any knowledge of the vernacular. . . . . We must abandon the vain dream that we can reproduce the English public school on Indian soil. We must recognise that it is a mistake to insist that a man shall not be considered to be an educated man unless he can express his knowledge otherwise than in a language which is not his own. Place no restriction on English as an optional subject, but cease to demand it as the one thing necessary for all."

And, I would add, having learnt English, use it as the key to all extra-Indian literature and culture; do not teach Greek or Latin unless in rare cases there is a reasonable prospect of the attainment of proficiency sufficient to ensure the enjoyment of the literature in the original. India has classic tongues of her own, the doors of culture for all who have the opportunity of passing beyond the merely bi-lingual stage of education, which should be the general goal.

What are the essentials in the Indian point of view, which for their intrinsic value, and in the interests of the manysidedness of human development, it is so important to preserve? Space will not admit of their illustration at any length, but these appear to the writer to be some of the ideals that must be preserved in any true education system for India:—

Firstly, the almost universal philosophical attitude, contrasting strongly with that of the ordinary Englishman, who hates philosophy. For every science school in India to-day, let us see to it that there are ten to-morrow.* But there are wrong as well as right ways of teaching science. A 'superstition of facts' taught in the name of science were a poor exchange for a metaphysic, for a conviction of the subjectivity of all phenomena. In India, even the peasant will grant you that "All this is *māyā*;" he may not understand the full significance of what he says; but consider the deepening of European culture needed before the peasant there could say, however blindly, that "The world is but appearance, and by no means Thing-in-Itself."

Secondly, the sacredness of all things—the antithesis of the European division of life into sacred and profane. The tendency in European religious development has been to exclude from the domain of religion every aspect of 'worldly' activity. Science, art, sex, agriculture, commerce, are regarded in the West as secular aspects of life, quite apart from religion. It is not surprising that under such conditions, those concerned with life in its reality, have come to feel the so-called religion

* There is of course a danger of a new kind threatening Indian education at present—the desire to restrict free development, and confine instruction to such subjects and books as are not likely to awaken the spirit of progress or revolt. This conspiracy—it is no less—can only be properly checked if the entire control of Indian education is assumed by Indians themselves. My suggestions are based entirely on this assumption.

that ignores the activities of life, as a thing apart, and of little interest or worth. In India, this was never so; religion idealises and spiritualizes life itself, rather than excludes it. This intimate entwining of the transcendental and material, this annihilation of the possibility of profanity or vulgarity of thought, explains the strength and permanence of Indian faith, and demonstrates not merely the stupidity, but the wrongness of attempting to replace a religious culture by one entirely material.

Thirdly, the true spirit of religious toleration, illustrated continually in Indian history, and based upon a consciousness of the fact that all religious dogmas are formulas imposed upon the infinite, by the limitations of the finite human intellect.

Fourthly, etiquette,—civilisation conceived of as the production of civil men. There is a Sinhalese proverb that runs, "Take a ploughman from the plough, and wash off his dirt, and he is fit to rule a kingdom." "This was spoken," says Knox, "of the people of Cande Uda (the highlands of Ceylon) because of the civility, understanding, and gravity of the poorest men among them. Their ordinary Plowmen and Husbandmen do speak elegantly, and are full of compliment. And there is no difference between the ability of speech of a Country-man and a Courtier." There could be said of few people any greater things than these; but they cannot be said of those who have passed through the 'instruction machines' of to-day; they belong to a society where life itself brought culture, not books alone.

Fifthly, special ideas in relation to education, such as the relation between teacher and pupil implied in the words of *guru* and *chela* (master and disciple); memorizing great literature,* the epics as embodying ideals of character; learning a privilege

* See "Memory in Education."

demanding qualifications, not to be forced on the unwilling, or used as a mere road to material prosperity; extreme importance of the teacher's personality.

"As the man who digs with a spade obtains water, even so an obedient (pupil) obtains the knowledge which lies in his teacher" (Manu II. 218). This view is antithetic to the modern practice of making everything easy for the pupil.

Sixthly, the basis of ethics are not any commandments, but the principle of altruism, founded on the philosophical truth: "Thy neighbour is thyself." Recognition of the unity of all life.

Seventhly, control, not merely of action, but of thought; concentration, one-pointedness, capacity for stillness.

These are some of the points of view which are intrinsic in Indian culture, and must be recognized in any sound educational ideal for India; but are in the present system ignored or opposed. The aim should be to develope the people's intelligence through the medium of their own national culture. For the national culture is the only *Aussichtspunkt* from which, in relation to a wider landscape, a man can rightly *sich am Denken orientiren.* To this culture has to be added, for those brought into contact with the modern idea, some part of that wider synthesis that should enable such an one to understand what may be the nature of the prospect seen from some other of the great headlands, the other national cultures, wherefrom humanity has gazed into the dim sea of the Infinite Unknown. To effect this wider synthesis, are needed signals and interpretations, rather than that laborious backward march through the emptiness of a spiritual desert where one may perish by the way, or if not so, then weary and footsore arrive at last upon one of those other headlands, only to learn, it may be, that there is to be found a less extensive prospect and a more barren soil.

As has been well said, Western knowledge is necessary for India, but it must form for her, (and especially for her women), a *post*-graduate course.

'Every man who is capable of judging' knows that the educational system of modern India requires re-casting. The task may be Herculean; the more reason to begin before it become impossible. The work must be done by Indian hands. It may be true, as Professor Geddes wrote to me lately, that

"The trouble is not only with the vested interests of the official class (which are sure to be protected in any change), but in the wooden heads, the arrested minds, the incompetent hands, etc., etc., of those who have gone through this machine, whether here or with you in India. It lies in your thousands of barristers and clerks and crammers, who know all the programme of the University of London in its darkest days. . . but who know nothing of the vital movements in literature, science, art, etc., by which we in some measure here escape or at least mitigate our official oppression, or even begin to modify it.

"In short, then, the strife is not between '*Eastern* and *Western Education*' (Instruction, Cram rather) but between *Cram* and *Education*, and for both alike, in West as in East. It is very hard indeed, upon *your* thousands of graduates to say that they must be considered as lost victims of a mistake, and put aside as useless for practical purposes, save here and there the man who has the will and power to re-educate himself; but the same is true here at home, and nothing could be more disastrous, I think, than for you in India to give your present Europeanised graduates the re-organizing of things; that would be continuing our mistake, not correcting it. But recover your own arts, etc., on one hand, and *utilise also the Western progress since* the futilitarian doctrinaires and their bureaucratic successors. Learn from France—non-official France primarily of course,—from America on her non-philistine side, from Germany at her best (though this is being materialised in most of the universities or elsewhere), from the small countries you as yet practically ignore—Scandinavia, Netherlands, etc., and so on. Don't believe the usual contempt of South American States; they are far more advanced than most Europeans know: in short, open yourselves more widely to the Western influence—*similia similibus curantur.*"

From such advice there is not a little to be learnt. But it is not true that any others can do for us the work that is our own; the re-organization of Indian education, if it is to be of any use, must be accomplished by Indian hands. The most denationalized Indian is still more Indian than a European. It is for Indians to nationalize Indian education. Given the responsibility, and the power to act, and even Europeanized India will rise to the occasion; to those who cannot think so, India must appear to be not worth the saving. Let Indians place the control of education in the forefront of the nationalist programme. By control, let absolute control be meant, not merely a half control, or a control sanctioned by some royal charter that may be withdrawn as easily as given. There is one true service, and one only, which England can now render to the cause of Indian education; it is the placing of the education budget and the entire control of education in Indian hands. It will then be for us to combine with our own national culture, all that we may learn from Denmark, Hungary, and the other smaller lands more educationally advanced than England, if it seems good to us to do so. It will be for us to develope the Indian intelligence through the medium of Indian culture, and building thereupon, to make it possible for India to resume her place amongst the nations, not merely as a competitor in material production, but as a teacher of all that belongs to a true civilization, a leader of the future, as of the past. Herein the ordinary English educator can help but little, and can hinder much. In the last words of Buddha to his beloved disciple:

"O, Ananda, be ye lamps unto yourselves; be ye refuges to yourselves. Hold fast to the *dharma* as to a lamp; hold fast to the *dharma* as a refuge. Look not for refuge to any one beside yourselves."

Memory in Education.

CHAPTER X.

"Few therefore are left who have sufficient memory."

PLATO, PHÆDRUS.

ONE of the most conspicuous features in Indian education as it used to be, was the training of memory. For long after writing was introduced, religious literature, history and technical knowledge were handed on orally from one generation to the next. Education, as in ancient Greece, was by means of oral instruction, and the learning by heart of classic literature. The learned man did not rely upon his library, but upon his memory alone. The memory thus trained and relied upon was capable of marvellous feats; even now there are men who know by heart hundreds and thousands of verses of Sanskrit literature which they have learnt once for all and can never forget. So too the singer of hymns or player of instruments used no written music, but relied altogether on memory; in the dark, or on a journey, it was all the same, what he knew was always at his command. Learning of this kind is growing rare; in India it has been generally superseded by the State systems of primary education.

Socrates, in the Phædrus, is made to relate the story of an Egyptian named Theuth, who invented numbers and arithmetic, geometry and astronomy, draughts and dice, and above all, letters. At that time Thamus was king of all Egypt. "To him Theuth went and shewed him his arts, and told him that they ought to be distributed amongst the rest of the Egyptians. Thamus asked him what was the use of each, and as he explained it, according as he appeared to say well or ill, he either praised or blamed him. Now Thamus is reported to have said many things to Theuth respecting each art, both for and against it, which it would be tedious to relate. But when they came to the letters, "This knowledge, O king," said Theuth, "will make the Egyptians wiser, and better able to remember; for it has been invented as a medicine for memory and wisdom." But the king replied, "O most ingenious Theuth, one person is able to give birth to art, another to judge of what amount of detriment or advantage it will be to those who are to use it, and now you, as being the father of letters, out of fondness have attributed to them the contrary effect to that which they will have. For this invention will produce forgetfulness in the minds of those who learn it through the neglect of memory, for that, through trusting to writing, they will remember outwardly by means of foreign marks, and not inwardly by means of their own faculties. So that you have not discovered a medicine for memory, but for recollection. And you are providing for your disciples the appearance and not the reality of wisdom."

The distinction between wisdom and knowledge must never be forgotten. It is wisdom which is the true end of education; in comparison with it, knowledge is a small thing. It is not a question of a useful as against a "fancy" education. It is one of point of view. Culture in the East has been only secondarily connected with books and writing; it has been a part of life itself. Knox tells us, in a passage which I have already quoted,* of 17th century Ceylon, that the "ordinary Plowmen and Husbandmen do speak elegantly, and

* p. 105.

are full of compliment. And there is no difference between the ability and speech of a Countryman and a Courtier." The Sinhalese proverb, "Take a ploughman from the plough and wash off his dirt and he is fit to rule a kingdom," was spoken, he says "of the people of Cande Uda. . . because of the civility, understanding and gravity of the poorest among them." *

How could this have been? It is explained by the existence of a national *culture*, not dependent altogether on a knowledge of reading and writing. I still take Ceylon as the special case. Think of a party of women spinning in a Sinhalese village, ten or twenty illiterate and superstitious country-women working at a common daily task; but they sang meanwhile, principally *Vessantara* and *Vidhura Jātakas*, the story of Yasodhara, or the struggle of Buddha with the powers of evil. The field labourer still sings of the exploits of Gaja Bāhu; or as he reaped the golden rice, the praise of some splendid *tala* palm; or a semi-religious song by moonlight on the threshing floor. Women still sing the story of

* So too with the Gaelic-speaking Highlanders of Scotland. "All were as courteous as the courtier" says Alexander Carmichael, almost in Knox's own words. One Hector Macisaac knew stories and poems that would have filled several volumes; he could not write, or speak any language but Gaelic, and had never been out of Uist; yet he "was as polite and well-mannered and courteous as Ian Campbell, the learned barrister, the world-wide traveller, and the honoured guest of every court in Europe. Both were at ease and at home with one another, there being neither civility on the one side nor condescension on the other. . . The people of the outer Isles, like the people of the Highlands and Islands generally, are simple and law-abiding, common crime being rare and serious crime unknown among them. . . During all the years that I lived and travelled among them, night and day, I never met with incivility, never with rudeness, never with vulgarity, never with aught but courtesy." How like Knox's description of Kandyan Sinhalese! But observe. "Gaelic oral literature was widely diffused, greatly abundant, and excellent in quality." And now courtesy and culture together are being civilised away. "Ignorant school teaching and clerical narrowness have been painfully detrimental to the expressive language, wholesome literature, manly sports and interesting amusements of the people" (in the Highlands of Scotland). Is not the same thing happening in India? And is the new education going to be any compensation for the old culture? Certainly few signs of such a thing have yet appeared. Were it not for the hope of 'change beyond change' we should be hopeless indeed.

Padmāvati as they weed in the fields. It is, thus, in the existence a common culture independent of the written word that we must seek the explanation of the classical character of even the colloquial language at the present day, which is emphasised by Prof. Geiger in his "Litteratur und Sprache der Singhalesen," (1901, p. 6.) where he prints side by side extracts from the *Ummagga Jātaka* in high and colloquial Sinhalese. So elegant indeed is some of the up-country Sinhalese still, that English-educated Sinhalese from Colombo are unable to respond in language of the same quality. This is natural enough, as Sinhalese and Tamil are usually not taught in the English schools at all, orally or otherwise.

It has not always been the case even in the West that education and culture were so much matters of book-learning only.

"Irish poetry" says Mr. Yeats, "and Irish stories were madeto be spoken or sung, while English literature, alone of all great literatures, because the newest of them all, has all but completely shaped itself in the printing press. In Ireland to-day the old world that sang and listened is, it may be for the last time in Europe, face to face with the world that reads and writes, and their antagonism is always present under some name or other in Irish imagination and intellect. I myself cannot be convinced that the printing press will be always victor; for change is inconceivably swift, and when it begins—well, as the proverb has it, everything eomes in at the hole. The world soon tires of its toys, and our exaggerated love of print and paper seems to me to come out of passing conditions and to be no more a part of the final constitution of things than the craving of a woman in child-bed for green apples.

"The old culture came to a man at his work; it was not at the expense of life, but an exaltation of life itself. It came in at the eyes as some civic ceremony sailed along the streets, or as one arrayed oneself before the looking-glass, or it came in at the ears in a song as one bent over the plough or the anvil, or at that great table where rich and poor sat down together and heard the minstrel bidding them pass around the wine-cup and say a prayer for Gawain dead. Certainly it came without a price; it did not take one from one's friends and one's handiwork; but it was like a good woman who gives all for love and is never jealous and is ready to do all the talking when we are tired.

"How the old is to come again, how the other side of the penny is to come up, how the spit is to turn the other side of the meat to the fire, I do not know, but that the time will come I am certain; when one kind of desire has been satisfied for a long time it becomes sleepy, and other kinds, long quiet, after making a noise, begin to order life."

In Ceylon the old culture has not entirely died out, especially in the up-country villages; it is however passing away, and in the most "civilised" districts is a thing of the past. This is partly due to the competition of Government and Mission schools, partly to the decay of Buddhism, partly to the general indifference to the importance of vernacular education. So much is the mother-tongue neglected and despised that instances of "educated" Sinhalese unable to speak to, or read a letter from, their own relations are by no means unknown; those who have been through the mill in an ordinary English school are usually very ignorant of the geography, history and literature of Ceylon. Most stupid of all is the affectation of admiring everything English and despising everything Sinhalese or Tamil; recalling that time in England when "Falsehood in a Ciceronian dialect had no opposers, Truth in *patois* no listeners."

The old system had, no doubt, its faults; but it did not divorce the "educated" from their past, nor raise an intellectual barrier between the upper classes and the lower. The memory system itself has many merits. It may be doubted whether the examination system, with its tendency to superficiality and cramming, is any great improvement. The most obvious fault of the Eastern memory system is the lack of provision for the development of the reasoning faculties and too great a reliance upon authority and precedent. But the examination system at present in vogue is also a memory system, and as such is inferior to the old,

I

inasmuch as information is merely got up for the immediate purpose and afterwards forgotten; this essentially temporary storage of facts has undoubtedly a weakening effect on mind and memory; the old-fashioned student at any rate remembered what he so laboriously learnt by heart; and this thorough knowledge of a considerable amount of real literature was in itself of no small value; through it he attained to what we call "culture." As Professor Macdonell has lately pointed out, "the redeeming feature of the native system, single-minded devotion to the subject for its own sake, is replaced by feverish eagerness for the attainment of a degree, through examinations which must be passed by hook or by crook." The examinations are not even good of their kind, for they make no provision for the history or languages of Ceylon, with the inevitable result that these subjects are neglected in schools. Under the old *régime* even those unable to read and write were often familiar with a great deal of legendary verse and ancient literature, and this general acquaintance with national literature produces a seriousness and dignity of speech foreign to the present-day youth. The grave Kandyan villager, ignorant of English and of the great world of business, was not lacking in courtesy and real culture.

Even the method of noisy repetition in the village schools (which indeed still characterises them) was not an unmixed evil. Scholars repeated their lessons "with a certain continu'd tone which hath the force of making deep impression on the memory" (P. della Valle, describing schools in the Deccan, 1623, quoted by W. Crooke). Sir Richard Burton says of such schools that their chief merit lies in the noise of repetition aloud, which teaches the boy to concentrate his attention! The "*viva voce* process is a far better mnemonic than silent teaching."

It is mainly however of older scholars that I speak, and of what they carry away from their education. An ordinary 'English' education may leave one with little capacity for self-entertainment, and does not give repose and dignity such as belonged to the old cultures of the East. Examinations do not do away with the necessity for learning by rote; they only make that learning of a temporary character. Does not every examinee know the relief with which, the pass list issued, he relaxes the effort to retain a mass of knowledge which he acquired only for the special purpose of that examination? I, for one, know it. One learns far too many subjects. I think no subject should be taken up which cannot be carried to some adequate length, no language studied by pupils who may not reasonably be expected to progress so far as to read the literature of that language with pleasure. It is extraordinary how easily what one learns for a purpose and not for its own sake is forgotten. I once passed the London Intermediate Arts examination in the various subjects, including Greek. In that Greek I took no real interest, and in less than a year after I could hardly spell out a few words, much less translate them. It was never supposed that I should become a Greek student; the Greek was part of a general education! But it did not teach me anything of the real Greece itself, its philosophy or art or literature. I came to read those later in translations, when the love of sagas led me to read Homer, and Indian philosophy led me to appreciate Plato, and Indian art led me to study Greek art too; and thus only did Greek culture come to mean anything to me. I studied Chaucer too; but not for years after did I know that Chaucer was pronounced differently from modern English and was beautiful poetry. There is thus something lifeless about English education by examinations even in

England; a tendency to study many subjects without reaching culture by means of any.

What this education becomes when imposed upon the East may be imagined. It was no doubt much easier to take the cut and dried curriculum, say of the Cambridge Locals, and apply it to Ceylon, than it would have been to study the local conditions, and make provision for education in the mother-tongues of the people, or the study of their literature. It would have been a laborious and difficult task (but how fascinating to one whose heart was in the work!) to examine Indian educational ideals, and embody them with the new ideas into a live scheme of education which should develop the people's intelligence through the medium of their own national culture. It would be a great undertaking now even to organize a University in Colombo, adapted to the needs of the Ceylonese.* It is infinitely easier to provide a scholarship in London. That may readily be granted; only those who shirk this labour and do not recognize their responsibility to the past, must not expect great credit for their labours in the cause of education. If Western education is to destroy, not to fulfil the ideals of the past, those who impose it cannot expect thoughtful men to welcome it.

I cannot think that European teachers and educationalists quite realise how far "English" education as it is given in the East is crushing all originality and imagination in the unfortunate individuals who pass through the mill. Yet the "Babu" and the "failed B. A." upon whom the Englishman looks down so contemptuously are the fruit of his own handiwork, the inevitable result of the methods of education which he himself has introduced. Broadly speaking, you take a people,

* Or to vitalise the Universities of India, the 'sordid and squalid' atmosphere of which is now fatal to all real culture.

and educate its children in foreign subjects, and do so in a foreign language, almost completely ignoring their own culture—and then are surprised at their stupidity! Suppose that England was governed by Chinamen, and a premium set on Chinese culture; English children taught Chinese subjects in the Chinese language, and left to pick up the English language and English traditions anyhow at home—would there not be some "failed mandarins?"

The question is really one of the evasion of responsibility. If Empire carries with it duties and responsibilities, as we are told by its apologists, a part of that responsibility is towards the already existing culture and ideals of the subject peoples. These ideals may be different from those of the rulers; upon these then is laid the hard task of conquering not only the subject race, but their own selves and their own prejudices. Men have no right to be intolerant of the ideals of others. And only those teachers can truly serve the East and especially India, who, "in a spirit of entire respect for her existing conventions and for her past, recognize that they are but offering new modes of expression to qualities already developed and expressed in other ways under the old training."

Even science is not everything; it is as easy to fetter the imagination with the bare facts of science, taught as knowledge, and not as wisdom, as to fetter it in any other way. Science is a poor thing without philosophy; and philosophy was a part of the old culture. The Buddhist books speak of the "three worlds," the world of desire (*kama loka*), the world of form (*rupa loka*), and the formless (*arupa loka*); to Buddhists these profound ideas are quite familiar. Of the idealism of the Upanishads, which permeates all Indian life and thought, Professor Deussen says that therein lie the roots of all religion and philosophy: "We do not know what revelations and discoveries are in store for the restlessly enquiring human spirit; but one thing we may assert with confidence,—whatever new and unwonted paths the philosophy of the future may strike out, this principle will remain permanently unshaken." The idealism of the Upanishads—which, is continually re-expressed in all Indian, including Buddhist, literature—is in marvellous agreement with the philosophies of Parmenides and Plato, and of Kant and Schopenhauer. And all this is an inseparable part of Indian culture as it was. The far-reaching character of these basic ideals of Indian culture have expressed themselves in an infinite variety of ways; but they are always there. Is not this culture worth saving? An English writer on Indian administration* remarks on the absurdity of the idea that "teaching Indian schoolboys a smattering of modern experimental science will be a revelation to a culture and a civilisation which constructed a theory of the Universe, based on what we call modern scientific principles, five thousand years ago."

It will be said that all this lies beyond the simple education required by many Indians, who have their work to do in the world, and have little need for philosophy. But the genius of the old culture was seen in this very thing, that *all* partook of it in their own measure; culture came to a man at his work, it was an exaltation of life, not something won in moments stolen from life itself. And one way in which this came about, perhaps the best and most universal way was through the literature; and that literature was mainly orally transmitted, that is, it was very much alive; it belonged both to the illiterate and to the literate; it expressed the deepest truths in allegorical forms which, like the parables of Christ, have both their own obvious and their deeper meaning, and the deeper meaning continually expressed itself in the more obvious,

* Havell, Nineteenth Century, June, 1907.

and both were beautiful and helpful. The literature was the intellectual food of all the people, because it was really a part of them, a great idealisation of their life; and what is most important of all, it was such as to be of value to all men; large and deep enough for the philosopher, and simple enough to guide and delight the least intellectual. So that all, however varied their individual attainments, were united in one culture, the existence of which depended largely on the existence of a living literature, forming an inseparable back-ground to daily life, known that is by heart. Just as the Icelandic family histories were the stories of lives lived in the light of the heroic stories of the North, so Indian life is lived in the light of the tales of India's saints and heroes.

The two great Indian epics have been the great medium of Indian education, the most evident vehicle of the transmission of the national culture from each generation to the next. The national heroic literature is always and everywhere the true basis of a real education in the formation of character. Amongst the Buddhists in Ceylon, the place of the epics has been taken by the stories of the life of Buddha and the legends that have clustered round his name. The value of the epics in education is partly in this, that they are for all alike, the literate and the illiterate, men, women or children; all are united in a common culture, however varying the extent of their knowledge. It is this common culture which the modern English education ignores and destroys. The memorising of great national literature was the vehical of this culture; and hence the tremendous importance of memory in education. For great literature of this kind, does not yield its message to the casual or unsympathetic reader at once, it must be part of the life of men, as the Greeks made Homer a part of their life, or the Puritans the Bible. It is no use to prescribe some one or two books of the Rāmāyana or the Mahābhārata, or a Jātaka for an examination course. No, the great stories in their completeness must be a means of the development of the imagination—a faculty generally ignored and sometimes deliberately crushed by present-day educators. The great heroic figures must express to us still the deepest, most religious things. For all purity is included in the purity of Sītā, all service in the devotion of Hanuman, all knighthood in the chivalry of Bhishma. "Such are some of the characters who form the ideal world of the Hindu home. Absorbed in her 'worship of the feet of the Lord,' the little girl sits for hours in her corner, praying, 'Make me a wife like Sita! Give me a husband like Rama!' Each act or speech of the untrained boy rushing in from school, may remind some one, half-laughing, half-admiring, of Yudhistira or Lakshman, of Karna or Arjuna, and the name is sure to be recalled. It is expected that each member of the family shall have his favourite hero, who will be to him a sort of patron saint, and may appear as the centre of the story if he is bidden to recount it. Thus, when one tells the Rāmāyana, Ravana is the hero; another makes it Hanuman; only the books keep it always Sītā and Rāmā. And it is well understood that the chosen ideal exercises a preponderant influence over one's own development. None could love Lakshman without growing more full of gentle courtesy and tender consideration for the needs of others; he who cares for Hanuman cannot fail to become more capable of supreme devotion and ready service. And justice itself must reign in the heart that adores Yudhistira.* "

Very great too has been the part which the *Purānas* have played in moulding Indian character.

* Sister Nivedita, 'The Web of Indian Life.'

I have often thought that not all the efforts of a hundred Moral Instruction Leagues and Moral Education Leagues can do for England what the Epics and the Purānas have done for India. The foundation of all true education lies in the national heroic literature. Poor, indeed, is the nation lacking such a means of education; and mistaken an educator who should dream of deliberately ignoring such a means of education laid ready to his hand in India!

Not less related to the fundamental realities of life is the epic literature of Buddhism, with which the people, literate or not, were familiar. For the cycle of Buddhist literature may fairly be called epic, with Buddha as its hero. Is not *all* sacrifice summed up in his renunciation of the attainment of Nirvāna, when as the Brahman Sumedha the Bodhisat preferred to pass on through yet more existences towards the attainment of saving knowledge for the sake of creatures? What can be more beautiful than the story of his temptation by Māra, beneath the bō-tree, deserted by even the devas, save only Mahikāntāva, Mother Earth herself? Or the way in which, when four bowls were offered to him by the Four Regents, he accepted all, making them into one, that he might not refuse the offering of any? For the Sinhalese Buddhist again, it is in the Jātakas and in the rest of the Buddhist classical literature that Indian culture and civilization are presented; the stories are of Benares and of the life of India long ago. The *Vessantara Jātaka* is a perpetual delight to the simple country people; they see it all before them, just as it is painted on the *vihāra* wall; do not they think of that sojourn in the forest, when they too go to make their pilgrimage to Samanala? Into their very mats are woven symbols of the *pansala* at Vangagiriya where Vessantara and Madri Devi dwelt! Many of the Jātakas are perfect stories. There is the *Chhadanta*, telling of the elephant that yielded up its tusks to the hunter, and of the queen that died of shame and grief when she saw her evil wishes thus fulfilled; there are beautiful tales like the *Sasa* and *Bhadda Sala Jātakas*, and amusing ones like the tales of the pandits in the *Ummagga* and *Vidhura-pandita Jātakas*. Is it not worth while to teach these to young people of every generation? Are they not good literature to be in the minds of the old folk?

But it is not only from the point of view of the thing remembered that memory is important in education. Memory, in the Indian view, is itself a most important part of personal character, associated especially with the ideas of self-control and mental concentration. "From wrath is confusion born; from confusion wandering of memory; from breaking of memory wreck of understanding; from wreck of understanding a man is lost." (*Bhagavad Gītā*). The memory stands for a man's grip upon himself; its loss is characteristic of a disintegration of personality.

I pass then to the kindred subject of concentration. Psychology is for India, the synthesis of all the sciences. As by clay everything made of clay is known, so all knowledge is founded on a knowledge of the self. How is this self to be controlled and focussed? Only by the power of concentration, the capacity for fixing the attention of the whole mind for more than a brief moment upon a single aim or thought. Try to do this, try for example to think of a triangle, to see it in your mind's eye, and nothing else but it, for say two minutes; unless you have practised concentration of thought before, you will not be able to do it, other thoughts will slip into your consciousness before you know it, and you will find that your mind has wandered from its object. But in any case you will realise what it means to be able thus to concentrate the thoughts at will, to rule and not be ruled by them. Thoughts are not guests to come and go of themselves; they must be chosen and invited, or turned away at will.

I will give an instance or two of the way in which this concentration enters into the ideal of Hindu culture, and of the ways in which it is learnt. A typical story in the *Mahābhārata* describes the shooting lesson of the young princes. A clay bird is the target. Each prince in turn is asked what he sees. One says "A bird;" another, "A branch with a bird upon it," and so on. At last Arjuna, the youngest, answers; "A bird's head, and in that head only the eye." "The moment" says a writer on Hindu life "of the telling of this story to an Indian child is tense with feeling. For it embodies the culminating ideal of the nation, inasmuch as concentration of mind stands among Hindus for the supreme expression of that greatness which we may recognize in honour or courage or any kind of heroism."

Here is an illustration of the way in which concentration is learnt by those brought up in the atmosphere of Hindu culture. A part of the *sandhya* or daily prayer of the Hindus consists in the mental repetition of certain prayers (mantras) a certain number of times, in many cases 108. This might easily become a mind-deadening mechanical process; but this result is carefully guarded against, and it is instead good practice in concentration. For one thing, the counting is much insisted on; for repetition without keeping count leads to mental vacuity. Let anyone, on the contrary, try to repeat any two lines of poetry exactly 108 times, and see whether it does not require mental concentration to do it without failure. With the *sandhya* prayers there are also associated physical practices, especially that of breathing, retaining and expelling the breath, while prayers are repeated a certain number of times; this cannot be done without intense attention.

Many of the prayers too are, it is to be noted, "affirmations" of a very positive and beneficial character, practically auto-hypnotic suggestions. It is not surprising that Sandow found his most receptive pupils in India; for they already understood the importance of throwing the whole mind into every effort, not taking it in slovenly fashion with the body alone. The *sankalpa* is a resolve to perform *sandhya;* a Hindu writer remarks that upon this strong determination of the mental effort depends the efficacy of the worship. If the mind is not put into the act, it is done mechanically and loses half its value. The same thing was insisted on by Sandow in his system of physical training.

A great and real responsibility rests upon those who control education in the East, to preserve in their systems the fundamental principles of memory-training and mental concentration which are the great excellence of the old culture. No doubt, as I said before, it will be a difficult and troublesome process to so combine and fuse the old ideals with the new as to preserve the best in each. It is *much* simpler to reject the whole past and replace it by methods already cut and dried and defined. Nevertheless unless the necessity for doing the reverse of this is recognized, the English educator must not expect that his work will be taken at his own valuation, but must look forward to a constant struggle with those who wish, and intend, to preserve whatever was best in the old culture, especially the old appreciation of the value of memory training (most of all in connection with the making of great national literature an organic part of the individual life), and of mental concentration. But as I have already indicated, the future lies not with the English educator in India, but with the Indian people and the National Movement. The responsibility of preserving and continuing the great ideals rests with these, and not with any foreign educator.

Christian Missions in India.

CHAPTER XI.

"Self-control is meritorious, to wit, hearkening to the Law of others, and hearkening willingly."

"There is no such charity as the charitable gift of the Good Law. (*Dhamma*)"—Asoka's Edicts.

"I do not strive with the world, but the world strives with me. A teacher of the truth does not strive with anyone whatsoever in the world."—(Saying attributed to Buddha.)

THE following remarks deal only with missionary endeavour to convert Hindus and Muhammadans to some form of dogmatic Christianity, without touching upon the question of missionary activity as it presents itself in other countries, or in relation to the primitive tribes in India, whose beliefs are purely animistic and outside the pale of Hinduism proper.

Two questions require separate consideration in any discussion of Christian missionary activity in India; these are, first, is missionary effort justifiable at all, and second, are the methods employed defensible?

The first question must be answered in the affirmative. It is natural and desirable that every thinking man, who feels himself to be in possession of some key to the solution of the difficult problem of life, should desire to share this knowledge with others to whom it is still unknown. All to whom personal religious experience has come with the force of revelation long to share the gladness of it with others. Every teacher, every disciple, every common man desires by argument and persuasion, or indirect influence, to impress upon others some of the ideas which are, or seem to be, peculiarly his own, and peculiarly important. Christianity, Buddhism, Socialism, Nationalism, Imperialism, have alike inspired their missionaries and gained adherents. Naturally it has been so; enthusiasm is contagious, and affirmation more constructive than negation. Rightly it has been so, for only by spreading the truth can the truth be known; and in the end truth prevails over error. The mistakes have arisen when the preacher has forgotten that no truth is complete or absolute, only relative. No religion possesses a monopoly, unless it be of the errors peculiar to itself. The garment of the soul must be various, in relation to individual nature and environment, no less than must the garment of the body. The Christian missionary is generally bent upon the regimentation of the garments both of soul and body.

Any man may prophecy; the African fetish-worshipper has a right to speak if he feels a call to witness to the truth within him. He has no right to complain if he is not heard. So with the Christian; he may ask, as a Salvationist is said to have done, "Friend, how is your soul?"; but if he receives the answer, "Thank ye, pretty well, Sir, how is yours?" he cannot be surprised, and ought not to be shocked. Still less ought he to proceed by force, social influence or bribery to coerce the answerer's convictions; least of all by insidious means to undermine his children's faith in himself and his belief. Such considerations do not weigh with the Christian missionary.

The Hindu and the missionary conceptions of toleration are poles apart. The missionary is bent upon destroying heathendom; there probably could not be found a Hindu desirous of destroying Christianity. For the Hindu, religious formulas are not absolute truth, but truth in a mythical and allegorical form; how should that which is infinite be compressed into the tiny vessel of a single dogma ? He may think his own allegory best, or the best for him ; it may be best for others, but it is not likely to be so for all ; and so while he is willing and even eager to explain his form of belief to others, he is not bent upon securing their acceptance of it ; what he looks for is belief, not *a* belief.

A missionary after a painfully intense discussion once exclaimed to me " The light that is in you is darkness." Of course, I never dreamed of thinking that of him. For him, light had to be filtered through glass of a familiar colour before it could be recognised as light. Forms of religion are like coloured glasses that we hold up to a light too bright for human eyes ; pure white light is the truth behind them all ; not seeing this, men say to each other : " That is not light shining through your glass ; the only light shines through mine." The whole endeavour to prove that the light in heathen belief is not the same light as in Christian is an appalling waste of energy, when the real need is to awaken men to the fact that there is a light at all. What devout Hindu or Musalman has ever doubted that ? The materialist is the true heathen.

Many missionaries know but little of Hinduism or Buddhism ; they have not time to study them ; as these faiths are not Christian, they must be wrong, —why enquire further ? The home supporters of Christian missions are even more in the dark ; an ardent advocate of missions told me once that " Hindus were Muhammadans and worshipped Confucius." But this is no impediment ; for as Schopenhauer in his Essay on Religion says : " One finds the ordinary man as a rule merely trying to prove that the dogmas of the foreign belief do not agree with his own ; he labours to explain that not only do they not say the same, but certainly do not mean the same as his. With that he fancies in his simplicity that he has proved the falsity of the doctrines of the alien belief. It really never occurs to him to ask the question which of the two is right,"—or whether both may not be right.

Hear this story which I have been told of a Jewish and a Christian religious leader. Both were sincere religious men, cultured and devoted. The Christian cordially welcomed all converts that came to him from other faiths, to be received into his own. The Jew, when Christians came, as many did, to be received into the Jewish church, said to them: "Why do you wish to be received? you wish to worship in our synagogues? the doors are open, do so when you will. You wish to keep our moral laws? do so by all means, you will be a better citizen. You want to conform to our ritual? what good will that do you? it is the traditional discipline of a race, unsuited to you and a useless burden for you. You wish to be born of Abraham? that I cannot give you. You say that I have taught you what is good? well, if so, go away and practise it and teach it in your own church."

Buddhism and Hinduism are themselves missionary religions. The Buddhist Emperor Asoka (272—B.C.) organized foreign missions on a truly magnificent scale. These were perhaps the most successful missions ever undertaken, for it was his support that "made the fortune of Buddhism, and raised it to the position which enables it still to dispute with Christianity the first place among the religions of the world, so far as the number of believers is concerned" (Vincent Smith). With all his devotion to the Law of Buddha, what was his attitude to other sects? It is summed up in this extract from one of his edicts: "All sects have been reverenced by me with various forms of reverence. Nevertheless, personal adherence to a man's particular creed seems to me the chief thing." In another edict he says: "The adherents of the several sects must be informed that His Majesty cares not so much for donations or external reverence, as that there should be a growth, and a large growth, of the essence of the matter in all sects. . . The growth of the essence of the matter, assumes various forms, but the root of it is restraint of speech, to wit, a man must not do reverence to his own sect by disparaging that of another man for trivial reasons." What then was the burden of Asoka's missions, what was the message he so desired to communicate to all, what did he understand by conversion? It was not a dogma at all; it was the "Law of Piety" (*Dhamma*): "The Law of Piety is excellent. But what is the Law of Piety? It requires innocuousness, many good deeds, compassion, truthfulness, purity" (Pillar Edict II). This, with an insistance upon the greater value of meditation than of ceremonial observances, was the gospel of Asoka's missions. 'Conversion' was a turning of the heart, not the acceptance of a formula. Such was the work of the greatest and most successful missionary the world has seen. Were the ideals of the Christian missionary similar, he might make fewer 'converts'—and more followers of Christ.

What of Hinduism? "If," says Mr. Grierson, "the *bhakti*-cult is to be counted as a form of Hinduism (and if it is not, there would be very few Hindus in India), few statements so inaccurate have been made as that Hinduism is not a missionary religion. Here we have a form of belief which actually lives upon its missionary work. It ignores all caste and condemns no religion as utterly useless, and ever since its foundation its converts have increased in geometrical progression. Every follower of the cult is, and if he is genuine, must be, a missionary. Nor is the missionary field confined to existing forms of Hindu belief. The common statement that no Mussalman can become a Hindu is disproved by the fact that some of the greatest

K

saints of the cult, men whose hymns are household words and are printed and sold by thousands, were converts from Islām. Others, such as Kabīr and Prānanātha, succeeded in forming important sects which absorbed many of the actual doctrines of that belief. As in Buddhism, what we may term the laity was not called upon to abandon caste or its old household worship."* The spirit of this mission work is expressed in Pratāpa Simha's *Bhaktakalpadruma*, which Mr. Grierson goes on to translate: "Somewhere it is written in the scriptures that he who taketh one that is averse and turneth him towards the Holy One, hath earned the fruits of a thousand horse sacrifices. . . . The pity of it is that so many who gain wealth spend not more of it upon the spreading abroad of the Gospel of Grace *(Bhāgavata Dharma)*. . . Therefore let every man so far as in him lieth, help the reading of the Scriptures, *whether those of his own church or those of another.*"

This also is the spirit of the Bhagavad-Gītā: "They also who worship other Gods and make offerings to them with faith, O Son of Kunti, do verily make offering to Me": "Howsoever men approach Me, even so do I welcome them, for the path men take from every side is mine;" "If any worshipper whatsoever, seeks with faith to do reverence to any form whatsoever, that same faith in him I make steadfast."

Per contra, the missionary teaches: "I the Lord am a jealous God; thou shalt have none other gods but Me."

In India any man may preach any doctrine even upon the temple doorstep. He may believe what he will, if only his practice do not undermine the

* Grierson, "The modern Hindu Doctrine of Works." J.R.A.S., 1908, p. 340.

structure of organized society.* There has never been a conflict between science and religion, for science has always been religious,† and religion philosophical. It is a debated question whether there has ever been serious religious persecution in India; it is certain that it was the regular practice of Buddhist, Hindu, and some Muhammadan rulers, not merely to tolerate, but to support all sects alike. Such tolerance the missionary uses to spread his own intolerance. His aim is to win souls for Christ; and for him no other duty, principle or right can be allowed to interfere with his efforts to accomplish this end.

The use of physical force‡ is now indeed rejected; but all that money, social influence, educational bribery and misrepresentation can effect, is treated as legitimate. With all this is often combined great devotion and sincerity of purpose; the combination is dangerous in the extreme.

* "Hindooism has never produced an exclusive, dominant, orthodox sect, with a formula of faith to be professed or rejected under pain of damnation." (Vincent Smith, 'Asoka,' p. 39).

† Especially mathematics and astronomy. For example, fractions with a zero denominator are considered by Bhaskarācarya. Such quantities can neither be increased or decreased by addition or subtraction of any finite quantity whatever; hence he says, they are similar to Ananta, or the Infinite in a Theological sense: "In this quantity consisting of that which has cypher for its divisor there is no alteration though many be inserted or extracted; as no change takes place in the infinite and immutable God at the period of the destruction or creation of worlds, though numerous orders of things are created or put forth." To the Indian student of mathematics such a remark is at once illuminating; it would seem out of place in the naïvely materialistic scientific text book of the West. As a Western Scientist wrote to me the other day, "Western science has a great deal to learn from Oriental philosophy."

‡ Missionaries in the last resort rely on force. This is notoriously so in China. "Force," says Lafcadio Hearn (quoted Modern Review, III, 234), "the principal instrument of Christian propagandism in the past, is still the force behind our missions. . . . We force missionaries upon China, for example, under treaty clauses extorted by war, and pledge ourselves to support them with gunboats and to exact enormous penalties for the lives of such as get themselves killed." It would be the same in India, did not Hindu tolerance (apart from 'India held by the sword') make it needless; but even Hindu tolerance may some day be overstrained. If it be intolerance to force one's way into the house of another, it by no means necessarily follows that it would be intolerance on the owner's part to drive out the intruder.

We come thus to the second question, the legitimacy of missionary methods. It is impossible in a short essay to cover the whole field of missionary activity in India. I propose to deal with two special points, *viz:* Education, and Misrepresentation.

The most subtle, and in a certain sense, I suppose, effective proselytizing agency in India is the Mission School. When adult conversion was found to proceed too slowly, it was decided to reach the children; hence the education bribe. The magic word itself stills opposition and enquiry; everyone is convinced that India needs educating,—it would be intolerant to deny to Christians a right to share in this noble work, impertinent to doubt their capability. A deliberate effort is being made to "keep the education of girls predominantly in Christian hands for perhaps a generation," as it is thought that "upon the character and extent of the education provided for girls during the next few years will depend the spread of the Christian faith amongst all the higher castes of India." * Let us see what this education of girls in mission schools implies.

The education is undertaken with an ulterior motive, that of conversion. The first qualification of a teacher is therefore good sectarian Christianity; but for educational problems,—in these it is only necessary that she should be interested as a means to an end. However, the qualifications next desired are the ordinary qualifications of an English school-teacher; and in some cases the teacher may even be an University graduate. Such persons are sent out after some preliminary theological training, to teach in, or to take charge of, a mission school for girls. It is sometimes not decided until nearly the last moment to what part of the 'mission field' the

* The East and the West, 1908, p. 104.

teacher is to be sent. In any case she is not prepared for her work of education by a sympathetic study of local ideas, culture and traditions; if she studies the heathen religion at all, it is mainly in books written by those who do not sympathize with, and therefore do not fully understand it. Upon arrival, she finds herself in an altogether unfamiliar mental atmosphere; and she has only her Christian dogma, and at the best a good English education on classical lines, as her resources. Unless she is to be a preaching missionary, which as a teacher she is not proposing to do, she will probably learn no more of the mother-tongue of her pupils than suffices to direct her servants; the mission is short-handed, and she has to devote her whole time to class work and management.

But suppose that by a rare chance (how rare I need not say) she belongs to the microscopic percentage of Europeans in India for whom Indian culture, literature, philosophy, art and music, have a real fascination. The more she knows of Indian culture, the less can she found her scheme of education upon it, that is, so long as she remains bound by honour and inclination to proselytize. For all Indian culture is essentially religious; the aim of art is to interpret God to man through the medium of the heathen mythology she has been sent out to destroy; music is most often the expression of man's love for God, expressed in the same terms; the epics, the fundamental moulding agencies of national character, are practically heathen Bibles; and Indian philosophy and religion are inseparable. So that however keen her educational instinct, she has but one course to follow,—to create a spiritual desert in which to plant the Christian dogma. The greater part of the educational work of a mission is thus destructive. To a girl in such a school one of three things happens: either she is true to the ideals of the home, and so absolutely out of sympathy with her teachers; or she is converted, and regards her parents as ignorant idolaters; or she pretends conversion for the sake of certain material advantages. Sometimes she is persuaded that both the religion of her parents and the new religion intended to replace it are alike superstitions. (With young men this happens oftener.) In neither case is she 'educated,' in the sense of being given the freedom of her own national culture, the only true standpoint from which she can, in relation to a wider world, educationally 'find herself.' She is demoralised ('unmannered') and rendered less, not more, fit to take her place in life amongst her own people.

Now the true work of education is not merely to impart this, that or the other information, or develope a particular intellectual aptitude; it is to build up character. This is a constructive work; but as we have seen, the object of the missionary is primarily: (and with his conception of the meaning of conversion must remain) destructive. Indeed it may be said of the two types of purely English schools in India, Government and Missionary, that the one ignores, the other endeavours to destroy, the ideals of the home. Under such circumstances the possibility of true education is reduced to a minimum.

Why then send our girls to mission schools? It is, I think, unwise. But some of us are so convinced of the importance of education that we are driven to take what we can get. In desiring for our girls the kind of education given in mission schools, it may be that we have accepted, at your valuation, that which has no value. It is true that Indian women are not even now uneducated or non-educated; but their education is highly specialised; it is rather culture than learning; it is not recognised as education by the modern world. The education of Indian women in the past fitted them to satisfy all the demands of a beautiful social ideal. Moulded upon the national ideals of character enshrined in the heroic and romantic literature familiar to Indian women, the beauty of Indian womanhood is beyond the breath of criticism. But the time has come when new demands are made upon the Indian people; in the national and civic synthesis in progress woman must play her part, as she has done in other syntheses before. Hence the need for an education no longer so exclusively specialised in relation to the home and to religion; the need for a scientific, geographical, historical synthesis. Recognition of this need has led to the desire for 'English Education.' Hesitation as to the real aims of the education offered has kept many from seeking it; it might have been well had it kept more, for too often have those who asked for bread been given a stone. Be that as it may, English education is now desired by many; that which purports to be this thing is offered at low rates in missionary schools.

India is poor. The average income of individuals is estimated at from 1½d. (official) to ¾d. (Mr. Digby) per head per diem. Can India afford to erect in a day such educational institutions as those of Newnham or Girton? India is hard put to it to pay for the education of her sons; and has also to wage a desperate struggle for national existence on any terms; and yet does find money for such institutions as the Ladies' College in Mysore, the girls' school of the Arya Samaj at Jalandar, and other educational work. It is true that by now, Indians might, had they been wise, have done more for the modern education of Indian women; yet all things considered it is wonderful that so much has been, and is being done. Nevertheless, for those who desire 'English education' for girls, it is still generally a case of the mission school, or nothing. The mission school is subsidised by the contributions of the supporters of missions all over the world, and can afford to offer the 'English education' at less than cost price. The bribe is then accepted. Not till India refuses to be thus pauperised by those whose aim is the destruction of her faiths, can she be free.

The *motif* of the parent is not always a pure desire for education; it is sometimes a desire, not elsewhere unknown, to get something for nothing; sometimes a wish for mere material advantage for the girls. "Education is valued in India," says the Archdeacon of Madras ('The East and the West,' Jan., 1908) "not so much because it is enlightening as because it is profitable," and the missionary provides the easiest and cheapest avenue to the attainment of it. The first statement, in so far as it is true of modern India, is in direct opposition to Indian tradition, and to all that is best in Indian educational ideals. But the missionary does not scruple to take advantage of the situation, as a keen man of business might take advantage of a rival. Such methods may result in brief success amongst the least Hinduized sections of society. They will not touch the heart of India! In Ceylon the Cambridge Locals are for a girl as good as a dowry; but they are not education, for they leave the girl ignorant of her own language, history and social culture. Europeanised parents desire their daughters taught accomplishments; Berlin woolwork to be framed on the parlor wall; 'a few strokes on the violin before she leaves;' a little strumming on a cheap piano; painting flowers, sometimes a little French. They learn also to wear shoes, and feathers in their hats, often also to eat meat. This of course is pure snobbery: but since 'Christian influence' not education, is the aim, these things must be provided; and it often happens that these *bourgeois* ideals are the teachers' very own.

The teaching of mere accomplishments to all girls, irrespective of talent, is in the West, to be correlated with the overstocked matrimonial market; piano-playing and foreign languages were supposed to attract the average man. In the East, the matrimonial market is not overstocked. Most of the girls in Christian boarding schools are recruited from the villages; they will not be called to any station in life different from that in which they were born; for them the first essential of education should be to fit them for the life they will assuredly lead, that of the mother of a family. But still accomplishments attract; piano-playing, crewel-work and English manners (or the lack of them) here also contribute to matrimonial bargains, and so the village parent is content to take some risks. Take on the other hand the case of the cultured man with daughters whom he desires to educate in the best way, and who understands what education means. I think of one such, a learned Hindu, a Cambridge graduate, who has travelled with his wife in Europe, and is intellectually the superior of all his associates in the Civil Service. There is as yet no Hindu school for girls where modern education is available; he does not wish to send them far away to Mysore or to England; and so he too sends his daughters as they grow up, one by one, to the C. M. S. Ladies' College, where they are duly prepared for the Cambridge Locals, taught Christian dogma, French, fancy work and the piano, besides the English mathematics and other subjects of value for which they really go. Out of school he has to arrange for their instruction in their own mother-tongue, in Indian music and literature. It will be seen that time thus already over-filled, is too much occupied for the Sanskrit he would like to have them learn. In this particular case the strength of home ties and of religious feeling render the possibility of conversion quite remote; but how far removed is the education offered by the would-be proselytizers, from that which would be of real value.

Alas for wasted opportunity! To share in the true education of the Indian women were indeed a privilege. Behind her are the traditions of the great women of Indian history and myth, women strong in love and war, sainthood, in submission and in learning. She is still a guarded flame, this daughter of a hundred earls. She has not to struggle for a living in a competitive society, but is free to be herself. Upon her might be lavished the resources of all culture, to make yet more perfect that which is already most exquisitely so.. ....You that have entered on the task so confidently, with the ulterior motive of conversion, have proved yourselves unfit.

Lay no blame on India for her slowness to accept the education you have offered to her women; praise her rather for the wise instinct that leads her to mistrust you. When you learn that none can truly educate those against whose ideals they are blindly prejudiced; when you realise that you can but offer new modes of expression to faculties already exercised in other ways; when you come with reverence, as well to learn as to teach; when you establish schools within the Indian social ideal, and not antagonistic to it—then, perhaps, we may ask you to help us build upon that great foundation. Not I trust, before; lest there should be too much for the daughters of our daughters to unlearn. I speak now of Missionary misrepresentations.

There is no part of the Christian code of ethics more consistently ignored in missionary circles, than the commandment, "Thou shalt not bear false witness against thy neighbour."

It has been said, "By their fruits ye shall judge them." Now if the fruits are grapes and figs, obviously the plants cannot be thorns or thistles. Hence the necessity for seeing and describing the fruits of Hinduism and Islam not as grapes or figs, but as something more appropriate to the missionary conception of the plant. The result is a relentless and systematic campaign of vilification of all things Indian. When I say, 'necessity,' I do not mean to say that the missionary quite deliberately falsifies the facts; on the contrary, he deceives himself as well as others; this is easy, for when the plant is already identified as a thistle, it is difficult to see figs upon it, even if they be there. The missionary is not aware of his false witness; he does generally present things as he sees them, but he sees through highly-coloured spectacles, which he removes when turning for comparison to inspect a Christian society at home. Thus he blackens India's name, in all good faith, if one may call it so, and with the best intentions.

Those who wish to understand the process should study missionary literature, attend meetings, or read what missionaries say of those who see India in a different way. The method is simple and even obvious: Indian society, being like all others, mixed good and evil, the missionary (by no means free from the ordinary prejudices of other Anglo-Indians) sees and describes only evil; much that is merely strange he mistakes for evil, or notices only because it is strange; much he argues from particular instances to be universal; and all he sets down to the vile nature of the Hindu religion or of Islām or Buddhism as the case may be. It is as if a Chinese visitor to England, courteously received, were to describe to his friends in Pekin, the effects of drink and poverty, agricultural depression, the overcrowded slums with their moral and physical results, sweated industries and dangerous trades, baby farming, street prostitution, the unemployed, and the idle rich, and ascribe all together to the vile nature of the Christian dogma. How easy it would be for him to do this has, by the way, been suggested by Mr. Lowes Dickinson, in his 'Letters of a Chinaman.' In just this way the missionary home on furlough preaches his mission sermon or gives his mission lecture; and the collection is swelled by the contributions of a sympathetic but uncritical congregation, not quite free from a suspicion of gratitude to God, that they are not as other (heathen) men. Missionary literature is similar. A typical volume is Miss Carmichael's 'Things as they are in Southern India,' from which I have already quoted. No volume could be a more impressive monument of the unfitness of the ordinary missionary to concern himself with the 'civilization' of India. When in another man's heart you can see only blackness, the fault is likely to be your own; when in another civilization you can see unutterable vileness, it means that you have not understood the parable of the mote and the beam. The method of such a book is simplicity itself; ignore the presence of virtues in non-Christian, and of vices in Christian, communities; describe all individual and local instances of evil known to you in a heathen society as typical; add violence of language and morbid religious sentiment, suggest all that you do not say, and the volume is completed.

I shall now quote some few examples of missionary mis-statements from various less extreme sources. Easily refuted, such statements perhaps do less harm, except amongst the most ignorant, than do those which contain some element of truth, or extend a local or particular instance to cover a whole race of country.

Here is a statement absurd upon the face of it, yet given as an absolute fact, without any qualification at all: "The Hindu Christian (*sic*), who is going to disgrace his family once for all by breaking caste through baptism, will be quietly poisoned by his nearest relative to avert such a catastrophe." Another statement in the same article perhaps explains the value of such a writer's evidence: "Students of non-Christian religions must consider Heathenism on its worst side, if only to counteract the sentimental fancies of some who chatter about 'the beautiful religions of the East.'" *

Take another kind of statement; Hinduism is said to have contributed to Indian poverty by making the arts degrading: "The civil architect is branded as a bastard. The carpenter and the goldsmith are accursed, because the Brahmans choose to take umbrage at them. How could the arts flourish in such a society?" † Sir George Birdwood may be allowed to answer this ignorant and stupid statement. He says of the Indian handicraftsman: "The cause of all his comfort, of his hereditary skill, and of the religious constitution under which his marvellous craftsmanship has been perfected is the system of landed tenure which has prevailed in India, and stereotyped the social condition and civilization of the country from the time of the Code of Manu." Again: "In the happy religious organisation of Hindu village-life there is no man happier than the hereditary potter." "The village communities have been the stronghold of the traditionary arts of India; and where these arts have passed out of the villages into the wide world beyond, the caste system of the Code of Manu has still been their best defence." ‡

I take an even more serious example of very special pleading, from a more widely-read volume 'Lux Christi §', published for the Central Committee of the United Study of Missions. This book

* "Heathenism as a Social Influence," by Mrs. Ashley Carus-Wilson, 'India's Women and China's Daughters'. January 1907, page 2.

† K. M. Banerjea, quoted, "The Fruits of Hinduism," 1893, page 3. (Christian Literature Society.)

‡ Birdwood, 'Industrial Arts of India,' I. 137 and II. 146.

§ 'Lux Christi, An Outline Study of India, A Twilight Land,' by Caroline Atwater Wilson, Macmillan.

in 1903, the date of my copy, and the year after first publication, had already been reprinted seven times; I do not know how often since. Here we read (p. 211):

> It should be borne in mind that the mighty systems of paganism in India, whether Hindu, Buddhist, or Muhammedan, are alike destitute of all those fruits of Christianity which we term charitable, philanthropic, benevolent. Where are the hospitals, dispensaries, orphanages, asylums for the leper, the blind, the deaf and the mute? They have no place in the heathen economy.

Such a statement hardly needs refutation; but since there must be persons able to believe it, let me answer it by quotations from a single volume, the Sinhalese Mahāvamsa.* King Duttha Gāmani (161-137, B. C.) on his death-bed could say:

> I have daily maintained at eighteen different places, (hospitals) provided with suitable diet, and medicines, prepared by medical practitioners for the infirm.

Buddhadāsa, (A.D. 339) was not only himself a physician, but "out of benevolence towards the inhabitants of the island, the sovereign provided hospitals for all villages, and appointed physicians to them. The Raja, having composed the work *Sarattha-sangaha*, containing the substance of all medical science, ordained that there should be a physician for every twice five villages, and set apart one-twentieth of the produce of fields for the maintenance of these physicians." Parākrama Bāhu (A. D. 1164-1197) built a large hall that could contain many hundreds of sick persons:

> To every sick person he allowed a female servant (nurse), that they might minister to him by day and night, and furnish him with the physic that was necessary, and with diverse kinds of food. . . . And he also made provision for the maintenance of wise and learned physicians who were versed in all knowledge and skilled in searching out the nature of diseases. . . .

* This particular lie has been more fully dealt with in the 'Dawn' Magazine, July and August, 1909.

And it was his custom, on the four Pohoya days ('Sabbaths') of every month, to cast off his king's robes, and, after solemnly taking the five precepts, to purify himself and put him on a clean garment, and visit that hall together with his ministers. And being endued with a heart full of kindness, he would look at the sick with an eye of pity, and being eminent in wisdom and skill in the art of healing, he would call before him the physicians that were employed and enquire fully of the manner of their treatment......also to some sick persons he would give physic with his own hands......unto such as were cured of their diseases he would order raiment to be given......In this manner indeed did this merciful king, free from disease himself, cure the sick of their diverse diseases from year to year.

Vijaya Bāhu (A.D. 1236) "established a school in every village." Such refutations could be multiplied indefinitely, but the association of charity with religion in modern India is too familiar to require proof. It is unfortunate that libels upon nations and religions cannot be punished as can libels upon individuals. At any rate, it is obvious that missionaries capable of making such statements are unfitted to be teachers in India; whether by ignorance or insincerity, it may be left to them to explain.

Commoner than the simple lie described above, is the half truth or misrepresentation. Many of these relate to the position of women. Sister Nivedita says that she has heard the following thirteen statements made and supported in a single speech; each statement has a familiar ring to the student of missionary literature. They were as follows:

(1) That the Hindu social system makes a pretence of honouring women, but that this honour is more apparent than real; (2) That women in India are deliberately kept in ignorance; (3) That women in India have no place assigned to them in heaven, save through their husbands; (4) That no sacramental rite is performed over them with Vedic texts; (5) That certain absurd old misogynist verses...are representative of the attitude of Hindu men to their women-folk in general; (6) That a girl at birth gets a sorry welcome; (7) That a mother's anxiety to bear sons is appalling; 'her very wifehood

depends on her doing so'; (8) That the infanticide of girls is a common practice in India; (9) That the Kulin Brahman marriage system is a representative fact; (10) That parents unable to marry off their daughters are in the habit of marrying them to a god (making them prostitutes) as an alternative; (11) That Hindu wedding ceremonies are unspeakably gross; (12) That the Hindu widow lives a life of such misery and insult that burning to death may well have seemed preferable; (13) That the Hindu widow is almost always immoral.

Such indeed, as I judge from personal experience, is the picture which a majority of professing Christians in England have formed of the life of their Indian sisters; they are helpless prisoners awaiting their release at the hands of chivalrous Western knights. To hasten that release they unselfishly contribute both their time, their money, and their prayers. No wonder it has been said that the Nonconformist conscience is a greater obstacle in the way of India's freedom, than even Imperial greed. It would be waste of time to give the answers to these thirteen statements here; but I may, as Sister Nivedita does, classify them. Nos. 1, 3, 7, 11 and 13 are entirely false; Nos. 2, 5 and 12 are the result of misinterpreting or overstating facts; Nos. 4, 8, 9 and 10 may be true of certain limited localities, periods, or groups, yet are spoken of as representative of Hindu life as a whole. The last class is the most important; take only one example, No. 8; it is true that infanticide was at one time common amongst a certain class of Rajputs; but "it is in no sense a common Indian practice, any more than, if as much as, it is a common London practice." Indeed, in almost all these cases, a terrible *tu quoque* can be alleged,—not to speak of vices peculiar to the Christian West.

I briefly review some other common missionary statements. The sacrifice of goats to Kali is condemned,—though they are slain at a blow. The scene is described in all its horror; the simple English audience is led to think of it as typical of heathendom; and to forget their slaughterhouses and their rabbit coursings, the 'accidents' that happen to the carted deer, and the young ladies of the country-house who assist at the death of carefully imported foxes, only too happy if the bloody tail is their reward for a successful chase. The mode of worship of Hindus and Buddhists is called idolatrous; whereas every missionary must know that this is in direct opposition to the statements of the Hindus and Buddhists themselves. This is not the place to enter into a discussion of the rationale of image-worship;* suffice it to say that the distinction between a symbol and a fetish is, to the Protestant missionary, nil. Hindu literature is said to be gross and impure; to those who see in sex-love merely the gratification of an animal passion, this may seem to be so, for certainly, like Shakespeare and the Old Testament, Eastern literature is not fettered by the conventions of Victorian England. Bishop Caldwell has said, "The stories related of Krishna's life do more than anything else to destroy the morals and corrupt the imagination of the Hindu youth.": but *honi soit qui mal y pense*, .. the stories of the child-Krishna delight the mother-heart of every Indian woman, the love of Krishna for Rādhā typifies to Indian men and women that ideal love which Dante felt for Beatrice, and the love of the soul of man for God; the teachings of Krishna in the Gītā, are the consolation and guide in life alike of the learned and unlearned, the 'New Testament' of Hinduism. Indian dress, again, is 'indecent'; we hear nothing of its beauty, freshness and refinement. But decency is not intrinsic in one part of the human body, and indecency in another; the Lord made them all, and saw that they were good. What constitutes decency at a given time or

* But see J. M. Nallasawmi Pillay's '*Sivagnana Botham*,' 1895, notes to sixth Sutra. (pp. 73, 74.)

L

with a given people is a social convention, the details of which depend on a variety of local causes. A number of English customs appear indecent to the Oriental who ignores this point; and it is a fact that the conventional Englishwoman's dress, with its strong sexual exaggerations (pinched waist, small shoes, uncovered neck, etc.) is far more indecent than any state of nature. But let not the hearts of Indian men, and women be troubled; there is no reason why Indians should dress in such a manner as to spare the tender susceptibilities of European visitors; the latter, if they are philistine enough not to see the beauty of our dress, may look the other way.

Of caste, only evil is spoken, its trade-guild and eugenic aspects being altogether ignored. It is related as horrible that men are divided into groups that may not intermarry; as if the situation were not almost identical in Europe, only there the rank depends more on wealth than on descent; and as if the missionary did not himself belong to the most arrogant of Indian castes, the Anglo-Indian. How many missionaries would care to see their daughters marry an Indian of any caste?

Finally we have the misrepresentation of Hinduism itself; or of Buddhism, or Islam as the case may be. "Sometimes," says an English writer "a faint suspicion....haunts us that Englishmen are constitutionally unable to realise the spiritual life of any other people." It is perhaps worth while to briefly illustrate both the ignorance of bare facts, and the incapacity to understand unfamiliar religious experience by one or two typical quotations from missionary books. One writer says:—

> The fundamental error of Hinduism is to judge God by our own standard. The doctrine of Maya is pure imagination, utterly opposed to common sense....Christianity on the other hand, affirms the reality of the universe, and the trustworthiness of our senses....Every one of our five senses....bears witness to the reality of the objects around us. To any man

endowed with a grain of common sense, the opinion maintained by some of the schools that the soul is infinite, like *akdsa* must seem the height of absurdity. Other views held are scarcely less extravagant, that it is eternal, *svayambhu*, self-existent. Not a single character in the Hindu pantheon, or in the pantheon of any other nation, has claimed the position of one who offered himself as a sacrifice for the benefit of humanity.

The author of 'Holy Himalaya,' a missionary book of the worst type, writes :

"Hinduism has no system of moral teaching, with definite sanctions or adequate basis."

It would be cruel to continue making quotations which illustrate the 'constitutional inability to realise the spiritual life of any other people.' Suffice it to say that those who suffer from it are not fitted to educate the Indian people, and it is questionable whether we do well to permit them to do so.

The question of our attitude towards the Christian missionary is not an academic one. His misrepresentation of India at home, and miseducation of Indians in India, do us serious injury by suggesting that it is England's God-given mission, not only to rule, but to civilise and to convert us, and by raising up a generation of 'educated' Indians who are indeed strangers in their own land. What is to be our course of action in relation to these facts? The answer is fairly simple. The power of the missionary at home to misrepresent is being continually lessened with the increasing knowledge of Indian religion and Indian civilisation contrasting so markedly with the indifference of even ten years ago. The funds of missionary societies in America were considerably lessened for a time subsequent to the speeches of Swami Vivekananda at the World's Parliament of Religions; "if that is what Hinduism means, why are we helping to destroy it? We wish to know more", they said. Just now in America, the keenest interest is now being taken in Indian religion and philosophy, and the tables are indeed

L 2

turned by the presence of Hindu missionaries in California and New York. In England progress has been slower, owing to political prejudice, an incidental illustration of the injury done, not only to ruled but to ruler, by the ownership of one nation by another. Yet there have recently been founded in London, both a Buddhist Society and a Vedanta Society. Still more significant is the ready market found for books on Indian thought: the 'Wisdom of the East' series published by Mr. Murray; the inclusion of the Gītā in Messrs. Dent's 'Temple Classics'; the publication in English of Deussen's works on the Vedanta. Then there are the writings of Sister Nivedita, of Mrs. Besant, of Fielding Hall; recent articles by Mr. Nevinson in the *Manchester Guardian*; and, not least, the strong sympathy of the Labour Party for Indian aspirations. Labouring classes are very little interested in missions; they know what 'Churchianity' at home means. Indeed the supporters of missions belong for the most part to particular sections of the middle class; and even these are becoming leavened by the New Theology, or have lost their interest in forms of conventional religion. The trend of Western science has been at first to make materialists; its philosophy is now more transcendental; either way, it has helped to educate Europeans away from proselytising ideals. And so, as far as misrepresentation is concerned,—it is not at all dead (we saw plenty of it at a recent missionary exhibition in London, where there was a daily pageant representing the 'bringing of light to the heathen'),—but it is slowly dying a natural death, and we may assist this process by making clear to the world what the ideals of Indian civilisation really are, and totally ignoring ill-informed criticism.

In respect of education, the remedy is almost altogether in our own hands. Let us cease to allow ourselves to be pauperised by sending our sons and daughters to schools supported by the contributions of those in far off lands who know nothing of us, but are quite sure that we are living in the deepest spiritual darkness. It is shameful for us to allow these worthy people to do for us, so badly, what we could (if we would) do so much better for ourselves. The subject of National Education is perhaps the most important of all before us, for it lies at the root of all other problems. There are already signs that the missionaries themselves are waking up to the fact that something different in the way of education must be given if they are to retain their present power and position amongst us. The healthy rivalry of Hindu and Buddhist schools in part accounts for this; the presence amongst the missionaries of a few men with serious educational ideals is another cause. Do not let us be behind them in the work. We must not rest content for a single moment until the whole of Indian educational machinery is taken out of the hands of Government and the missionaries, to be controlled by ourselves. And as at present so many of us are almost as unfitted by the existing systems of so-called education as the missionaries themselves to do this work, let us prepare ourselves for it, (as Professor Geddes suggests so forcibly in a letter quoted above) by studying the most important educational movements going on in the West, and especially by studying the educational systems of small and important independent nations, such as Denmark, Hungary; but above all by deeper knowledge of our own country, which contains within itself all the elements of a cult more profound and a faith more reasoned than that of any other land.

A most clear recognition of the true character of missionary activity, and a most determined resistance to its aims and methods are needed now. The author of 'Holy Himalaya' writes:

"The true friends of India are those who would change its root ideas.... the bogey of religious neutrality.... will have to be laid to a considerable extent...else in the end we shall have to make the confession that we as a nation have no rational objects in India beyond commercialism and exploitation."

It has been well said that the nonconformist conscience is the greatest barrier to Indian freedom!

In a recent number of the *School Guardian*, the editor refers to the Church Missionary Society's school at Srinagar as follows:—

"1,400 boys—mostly Hindus and a large proportion of them of high caste—are being changed from superstitious, cowardly, idle, and untruthful beings into manly Christians."

As a commentary on these characteristic statements, and in illustration of the effects of the policy they reflect, the following extract is given here, from an article by Lala Har Dyal.

"The missionary is the representative of a society, a polity, a social system, a religion and a code of morality which are totally different from our own. He comes as a belligerent and attacks our time-honoured customs and institutions, our sacred literature and traditions, our historical memories and associations. He wishes to give us a new name, a new place of worship, a new set of social laws. He has declared war to the knife against everything Hindu. He hates all that we hold dear. Our religion is to him a foolish superstition: our customs are the relic of barbarism; our forefathers are to him black heathens condemned to burn in the fires of hell for ever. He wishes to destroy our society, history, and civilization. Our Shastras, Darsanas and Vedas are for him so much waste paper. He regards them as monstrous machines devised by misguided priests to prepare millions for damnation in the next world. He condemns our manners, pooh-poohs our holy love, laughs at our heroes and heroines and paints us as black as the devil to the whole civilised world. He is the great enemy of the Hindu people—the Principle of Anti-Hinduism Incarnate—the Ravana of to-day who hates all that we cherish, despises all that we revere, all that we are prepared to defend with our very lives......

"He looks forward to the time when the Smritis shall be unknown to the descendants of present day Hindus, and the Ram Lila shall have become a meaningless word in their ears. He shall cover India with acres of burial-grounds; cremation is anathema to him. He is the arch-enemy who appears in many guises, the great foe of whatever bears the name of Hindu, the ever-watchful, ever-active, irreconcileable Destroyer of the work of the Rishis and Maha Rishis, of that marvel of moral, intellectual and civic achievement which is known as Hindu civilisation. Let us labour under no delusions on this point. You may forget your own name; you may forget your mother. But do not for a moment forget the great, all-important, outstanding fact that the missionary is the most dreadful adversary you have to meet....the greatest enemy of dharma and Hindu national life in the present age."

In these words there may be exaggeration—they do not apply throughout to the work of every missionary; but there is nevertheless essential truth; and it is resistance in this spirit which missionaries must expect in the future, if they persist in their mistaken aims and methods.

Is there to be no salvation then for the Christian Missionary, no place found for him in our ideal? Not quite so, perhaps. No church or sect can presume to say that its presentation of Divinity to man is complete or perfect; were that possible, Divinity must be itself as finite as the doctrine. It is true that there is ample work for missionaries in their own so-called Christian countries: but there is work for them in India too: "He that taketh one that is averse, and turneth him towards the Holy One, hath earned the fruits of a thousand horse sacrifices........Therefore let every man so far as in him lies, help the reading of the scriptures, whether those of his own church or those of another." Let them in this spirit help us both to restore, and to build upon the religious ideals of the past, not to destroy them; and, so coming, they will not lack a welcome from a people so serious and so religious as the people of India.

A time will come when Christian missions, as at present understood, will seem to Christians as wide a departure from the true spirit of Christianity as the crusades appear to us to-day.

Meanwhile, the missionary must not be allowed to 'educate,' until he really understands the Indian people and desires to help them to solve their own problems in their own way; he must not be allowed to teach, until he himself has learnt.

Swadeshi.

CHAPTER XII.

THE word *Swadeshi* means literally 'Own Country' and has been used in recent years in India to denote that side of the national movement which aims at making India, to a far larger degree than is at present the case, self-contained and self-sufficient, especially in respect of industries and manufactures. Briefly expressed, the object of the movement is to check the drain on Indian capital involved in the purchase of imported goods, by manufacturing the said goods locally; replacing the removal of money from Indian shores, by a circulation of money within the limits of India herself.

So far so good. But there have been manifested certain weaknesses in the movement, perhaps unavoidable at first, which it is the intention of the present chapter to discuss. Let us consider for a moment the nature of manufactured goods. We may from the Indian point of view divide them in two ways:

(1) into (a) things which are worth having, and (b) things which are not worth having; and

(2) into (a) things for the manufacture of which India is well adapted by natural resources, national temperament, or existing tradition, and (b) things which other countries are better able, for analogous reasons, to produce or manufacture.

It will be found, that, to a great extent, the classes (1) a and (2) a, and (1) b and (2) b, have a common application. The imitation of European ways of living, whether in respect of dress, food, architecture or what not, has led to the adoption of many European luxuries which are quite unnecessary, and sometimes positively injurious. We shall certainly be much wiser to do without these useless or injurious things altogether—with economy to ourselves—than we should be in making them locally, even worse than they are made in Europe. There is for example a large class of goods, cheap and nasty, which are manufactured solely for the Eastern market, and which no one with education or taste would use in England. Yet these are purchased eagerly by Indians who desire to furnish in the European style, and in such quantities that their drawing-rooms are more like shops than living-rooms. Not long ago an Indian Prince consulted an European friend as to the furniture in his palace. He said, 'Look here, you are an old friend, I want you to go through my palace and reject everything European which is not worth having, and which only excites the ridicule of Europeans.' The result was that over two lakhs worth of rubbish was sold in Calcutta. It would be difficult to say how many lakhs worth would be disposed of if a similar process were carried out on a wider scale.

Probably ninety per cent. of European articles purchased by Indians are either ugly or useless or both. The rich offend as badly as the poor, indeed more so, as they can afford to buy a larger quantity of useless and ugly things. All of these things cost money, and it is a waste of money not merely because the money goes out of India. It is a spending of substance for 'that which is not bread.' We shall certainly gain nothing by transferring the seat of their manufacture to India.

Humanity is not in want of manufactures. "Already, all over the world, man is labouring beyond all reason, and producing beyond all demand.. ... Longer, harder toil for the producer, frenzied, criminal extravagance in the consumer, these are the dired results of the development of manufacturing industries, which tends constantly towards increased production and lower prices."—(Max Nordan) This is not civilisation; this not the art of living. Civilisation consists, not in multiplying our desires and the means of gratifying them, but in the refinement of their quality. Industry *per se*, is no advantage. The true end of material civilisation is not production, but use; not labour, but leisure; not to destroy, but to make possible spiritual culture. A nation which sees its goal rather in the production of things than in the lives of men must in the end deservedly perish. Therefore it is that the Swadeshi movement, a synthesis of effort for the regeneration of India, should be guided by that true political economy that seeks to make men wise and happy, rather than merely to multiply their goods at the cost of physical and spiritual degradation.

Take one or two examples of Indian imports of European haberdashery. India imports over 187 lakhs value annually. What does this mean? It means woollen caps and leather shoes for infants, hats, ties, and collars for men, sometimes even corsets for women, and, if not that, at least safety-pins and ribbons and high-heeled shoes, besides English curtains and carpets for our homes. All this results merely from the mistaken idea of imitating others, in other words, from the attitude of snobbery which not long since was spreading through 'educated' India like a gigantic fungus. The immediate point to be considered here, however, is merely economic; an enormous sum of money per annum might be saved in India by returning to the simple ideas and plain living of our forefathers. There is, then a Swadeshi, a higher Swadeshi, which should boycot certain goods, not because of their foreign origin, but because of their intrinsic worthlessness. Take another class of miscellaneous goods, such as nibs, stationery, scientific instruments, clocks and watches, and a large part of machinery in general and many of the things made by it. Some of these things have with great difficulty been produced in India. But in such cases the quality of the locally manufactured article has been altogether wretched. The patriotic Swadeshist has to pay more for an inferior article. Now I say that, in the face of this state of affairs, it is no use having Swadeshi manufactures unless the home-made things are at least as good as the imported ones, and unless the people of India are benefited by their manufacture.

Take for example textiles, which are a speciality of the Swadeshi movement. Here we have clearly something which India has formerly excelled in producing, and still produces in large quantities. But the most vulgar Manchester prints are still fast driving out locally made and artistic materials. At the Madras exhibition of 1903, says Mr. Harris, "side by side with the very many good examples displayed in various textiles, there were a number of specimens of gaudy-coloured goods of weak design, colour and quality, poor imitations of art fabrics and European textiles." Why, then, do people stand with folded arms and look at a declining industry *in which there is money* without any attempt, in a practical way, to revive the trade? "Already a change for the worse is visible in the tastes of the common people, and one has only to go into any street or village near a large town to see the glaring cloths of Manchester or German production freely worn by the populace. These are rapidly taking the place of the beautiful white and tinted cloths of hand-loom work, so lately in general use all over India, and so much of which was, until the middle of the nineteenth century, exported to various countries." The Swadeshi movement has created a new demand for India-manufactured textiles. This has been a true instinct, but the essential weaknesses of the Swadeshi ideal, as hitherto conceived, have limited the value of the result. It matters very little to the village peasant whether his work is stopped by the competition of factories in Lancashire or in Bombay, or whether a few Indian or a few Manchester mill-owners get rich quickly. Just what the factory system is beginning to mean for India may be guessed from some details and extracts from the recent report of the Indian Factory Commission. In daylight mills the average working time for the whole year is 12 hours and 5 minutes; in mills fitted with electric light, 13-13½ hours; but the Commissioners say "in some provinces the law is ignored to an extent not hitherto imagined." The law referring to the half-hours recess, "is generally disregarded in rice-mills, ginning factories, presses and flour mills throughout India."

A writer in the Modern Review for October, 1908, commenting on the Report, makes the following extraordinary statements regarding women's work:

"Coming to the restrictions imposed upon the employment of women by the present Act, the Commission very fairly and reasonably opine that they are neither suitable to the operatives nor to the employers. That has been the general experience of all factory owners who have to employ a large number of females. In Bombay it is seldom the case that they have to work for more than ten hours a day. *So that they have no need to avail themselves of the ½ hour's mid-day rest prescribed for their benefit by the existing act.* In practice it has been proved beyond cavil that the women prefer to come late to their work and continually work at their winding or reeling machines for the whole time that they wish to work, generally from 7 a.m. to 5 p.m. v. c." Italics are mine.

I quote this statement to show what modern India is prepared to accept for the sake of commercial 'progress.' Those familiar with the factory system and its results, in Europe, and the resistance made to regulation and inspection, will be able to read between the lines, and to understand how mistaken India will be if she believes that the agitation for factory regulation is engineered from Lancashire "for the purpose of arresting as far as possible the progress of the cotton industry," by placing restrictions on the indigenous labour employed. It is of no consequence to India whether or no an agitation be engineered in part from Lancashire, or not; what is of consequence to her is whether or no the problems of physical and moral deterioration, overcrowding, drunkenness and unemployment, characterising the development of the commercial system in the great cities of the West, are to be imposed upon the East as well. That there is only too much reason to fear such a result, while there is too little to hope that Indians are any more alive to the danger than Europe was fifty years ago, is evident by other statements in the Report. It appears that in Bombay the operatives inhabit slums of the most wretched character, crowded and insanitary. The rent of a room 12 × 10 × 9 ranges from 2 to 5 Rupees a month, the wages of an ordinary 'hand' being from 7 to 18 rupees a month. They remark that the consumption of liquor among factory workers is undoubtedly greater than among men of the same rank in life engaged in other occupations. The Commission appear to regret that the operatives are still very largely connected with their villages, and are not entirely dependent on factory work!

"There is as yet", say the commissioners, "practically no factory population, such as exists in European countries, consisting of a large number of operatives trained from their youth to one particular class of work and dependent upon employment at that work for a livelihood....Matters however, are gradually improving; the standard of living is undoubtedly rising all over India, though slowly; and there are some indications that a class of factory operatives, detached from agricultural and village life, and depending largely or solely upon industrial employment, is beginning to be formed." "This," remarks the writer already quoted, "is a happy augury of the future physical and material welfare of operatives."

It is indeed sad, for anyone acquainted with the mature developments of industrialism in Europe, the 'town and country' problem, the filth and squalor of manufacturing centres,* and the now increasing desire to once more relate the life of the people to the land, to see India thus light-heartedly plunging into inevitable suffering of the same character.

"It may be," says Mr. Havell, "that legislation, by imposing restriction on the hours of labour and improving sanitary conditions, may check the rapacity of mill-owners and shareholders, and it may be that the latter in their own interests will some day do as much for their employees as wise and considerate men do for their horses and cattle, but even the wisest and most humane cannot in the pursuit of the ideal of cheapness make the modern system of labour, in power-loom mills, otherwise than intellectually and morally degrading. Nor can they remove the even greater evils which the system brings with it—the overcrowded, filthy, air-polluted cities, the depopulation of rural districts and the struggles between capital and labour which in Western countries constantly threaten the very foundations of society."

It is indeed astonishing to find in Bengal that politicians have supported the very un-swadeshi system of power-loom mills. It is true that the

* "It may well be the case, and there is every reason to fear it is the case, that there is collected a population in our great towns which equals in amount the whole of those who lived in England and Wales six centuries ago; but whose condition is more destitute, whose homes are more squalid, whose means are more uncertain, whose prospects are more hopeless than those of the poorest serfs of the middle ages and the meanest drudges of the mediæval cities." Thorold Rogers "Six centuries of Work and Wages," p. 46.

boycott of foreign goods has incidentally brought renewed prosperity to the hand-loom weavers; but it is only too evident that in many cases the principle of Swadeshi has been conceived of merely as a political weapon, rather than as the true basis of the re-organization of Indian life, and the means of bringing not merely wealth, but happiness to the Indian people.

I take musical instruments as a further illustration. The manufacture of Indian instruments is a decaying industry. Thirteen lakhs of rupees annually are spent on imported instruments—pianos, violins (including mechanical ones) and harmoniums and gramophones, the universal popularity of which is ample testimony of the degradation of Indian taste in recent times. And so while small Indian capitalists are in a position to exploit the national sentiment by making wretched imitations of good English paper, nibs, or soap, the skilled craftsman, in this case the maker of musical instruments, is starving for want of occupation, and his hereditary knowledge, a definite asset in the national credit, is passing away for ever. While groups of well-meaning individuals are busy making bad Swadeshi biscuits, and others sacrifice a few pice per pound to buying them, the carver of wood, the ivory inlayer, the drawer of wire and the professional musician are all neglected for the travesties of music performed on harmoniums or lily flutes, or reproduced *ad nauseam* on gramophones, the profit on whose manufacture goes out of India. Not that it would be any advantage to make them locally. The hope of reviving trade by reproducing locally any article that may come into fashion, without regard to its real value, is as delusive as it is mean. It is never an advantage to a nation to produce useless or vicious luxuries; it does not increase the national wealth. By the time your harmonium factory is doing well, and Indians in it, working seventeen hours a day, are producing for the shareholders a dividend of 35 %, or more (as in the Bombay cotton mills), some European or American invents a 'harmoniola' or something equally insane, cheaper and easier to play,—and where are you then? But no foreigner could make for you a *vina*, or paint or inlay it with ivory, or carve for it a figure of Sarasvati; those are things which European or American factories cannot do.

It is just so with other arts and industries: we neglect what lies at our doors, to buy from afar what we do not understand and cannot use to advantage. No wonder that we are poor; aesthetic demoralisation and commercial failure will always be inseparable in the long run. Cast aside the village weavers traditional skill, not only in technique but in design, and you destroy so much of the national culture, and the whole standard of living is ultimately lowered. Competition with Europe, on the lines of modern commercialism must involve intellectual, and ultimately industrial, ruin. It matters little whether it is the Lancashire manufacturer or the great millowner of Bombay who successfully contests the village weaver's market.

Men will do more for a sentiment or an ideal than they will for a material advantage. But the sentiment must be real and definite. At present it is the weakness of the Swadeshi movement that the arguments put forward in favour of it so often appeal to a purely material ideal of prosperity. I have sought in vain for any expression in Swadeshi writings of a primary desire to make goods more useful or more beautiful than those imported, or to preserve for the country any art, *qua* art, and not merely as an industry. Indeed, such statements can be found, but they have come from the mouths not of nationalists, but of Imperialists like Sir George Birdwood, and Lord Curzon!

M

In India the primary aim of at least a certain section of the Nationalist party, has been to compete with Europe in cheapness. But the idea of learning just enough of Western science or Western manufacturing methods to be able to undersell the imports at any given moment is as delusive as it is mean. Some more constructive aims and methods are needed if Indian manufactures are to recover their lost status, and if India is to avoid even some of the horrors associated with modern industrial production in the West.

Do not then let us compete with Western Nations by evolving for ourselves a factory system and a capitalist ownership of the means of production corresponding to theirs. Do not let us toil through all the wearisome stages of the industrial revolution—destruction of the guilds, elimination of small workshops, the factory system, *laissez faire*, physical degeneration, hideousness, trusts, the unemployed and unemployable, and whatever may be to follow. We may perhaps not think of these things now, we may be too much concerned with the political problems of to-day. But if we are wise, we, who want India to be free, must bethink ourselves that, when that freedom comes, these problems will be with us still; the possibility of their solution depends on foresight and wisdom now. The history of the industrial revolution in Europe has been a long and sad one, and only now, and slowly, are some of its worst results being recognized, and their remedy devised. That this industrial revolution was in a sense inevitable may be granted, and it may also be that at least the outlines of it must be imposed upon the development of the social organism in the East as well as in the West; and indeed, not only in Japan, but also in India we see the process already at work. But it is probably possible for Eastern nations to run through some of its stages quickly, and with the experience of other nations as their guide, to avoid some of the worst evils. The Japanese, who are sometimes as much in advance of Europe as India is behind it, have shown, in spite of the great disorganization and vulgarisation of their national life that has taken place already,* some signs of this pre-vision. In 1885 the Japanese Government arranged for the establishment of silk-guilds by the local authorities; one of their chief functions was to preserve the standard of production. There are nearly 129 such guilds at present.† It is also stated, says Mr. Havell, in the *Indian Trade Journal* of February 16, 1907, that the Japanese, in preparing to compete with European nations for commercial prosperity, are showing a distinct reversion to former ways and methods; amongst other things steps were being taken to reorganise the old trade guilds. The *Trade Journal* comments: "As the various Guilds grow in power and influence they will be able to dictate to European and American traders, unless the latter also enter into combination."

It is absolutely necessary for Swadeshi in India to be a foresighted and constructive movement if it is to be of ultimate and real benefit to the Indian people. The gaining of a temporary trade advantage, though valuable as a political weapon to-day, is a small matter compared with the ultimate development of Indian society.

It is true that there exist the germs of regeneration in the West; the ideals of democracy and socialism (equality of opportunity) must sooner or later be in some measure attained; and a time will come again, or the hopes of civilisation are vain indeed, when there will be for all men, work worth

* Someone has said that 'a typical modern Japanese is a hybrid creature, either an intellectual bastard, or a renegade devoting his fine intelligence to the old standard of his country'.

† M. N. De, 'How sericulture is encouraged in Japan.'—Modern Review, Oct. '09.

M 2

doing, a life not over-hard or over-anxious. and such surroundings as are fit for human beings. We are little in touch with these regenerative tendencies. It does not even follow that the situation must be saved for us in just the same way. But many of these ideals were already attained under the industrial systems prevailing in India. Each caste or trade possessed an organisation largely socialistic in character and embodying democratic and communistic ideals. It may well be doubted whether the true hope for Indian industry does not lie in some such developments of the caste system itself, in the village and home industries of the past, aided by such improvements as are needed (*e. g.* the fly-shuttle or the distribution of electric power).

No doubt a great many common things must be made by machinery in future; and it may even be that a time will come when machinery will be actually used as a labour saving, and not as a profit making device; but it is probable that men will not ultimately rely nearly as much upon machinery as is supposed; and where they must, or at any rate now do so, we may for the present very well leave other nations to do such hewing of wood and drawing of water for us, and concern ourselves with the revival, both for our own use and for export, of what are really our own industries, now decaying everywhere for lack of intelligent encouragement.

Not infrequently the Swadeshi cry is an exhortation to self-sacrifice. It seems to me that this is an entirely false position. It is never worth while in the long run putting up with second best. Swadeshi for the very poor may mean a real sacrifice of money. But how far this is really the case is very doubtful. If one should regard a standard of simple living, conditioned by quality rather than quantity of wants, where durability of materials was preferred to cheapness alone, it is fairly certain that even the peasant would be better advised to use (real) Swadeshi than foreign goods. And for those better off, for those who have adopted pseudo-European fashions and manners to talk of Swadeshi as a sacrifice is cant of the worst description. It implies entire ignorance of India's achievement in the industrial arts, and an utter lack of faith in India. The blindest prejudice in favour of all things Indian were preferable to such condescension as that of one who casts aside the husks and trappings of modern luxury, to accept the mother's exquisite gifts as a 'sacrifice.'

Not till the Indian people patronize Indian arts and industries from a real appreciation of them, and because they recognize them not merely as cheaper, but as better than the foreign, will the Swadeshi movement become complete and comprehensive. If a time should ever come—and at present it seems far off—when Indians recognize that "for the beautification of an Indian house of the furniture of an Indian home there is no need to rush to European shops in Calcutta or Bombay," there may be a realisation of Swadeshi. But "so long as they prefer to fill their palaces with flaming Brussels Carpets, Tottenham-court-road furniture, cheap Italian mosaics, French oleographs, Austrian lustres, German tissues and cheap brocades there is not much hope." When will Indians make it possible for an enemy to throw in their teeth a reproach so true as this?

Even more important, then, than the establishment of new industries on Indian soil, are the patronage and revival of those on the verge of extinction, the purification of those which survive in degraded forms, and the avoidance of useless luxuries, whether made in India or not. Swadeshi must be inspired by a broad and many sided national sentiment, and must have definitely constructive aims; where such a sentiment exists, Industrial Swadeshi will be its inevitable outcome without effort and without failure.

CHAPTER XIII.

Indian Music.

"We have harmonies which you have not, of quarter sounds, and lesser slides of sounds: divers instruments likewise to you unknown, some sweeter than any you have."

BACON'S *New Atlantis*.

"The introduction of a new kind of music must be shunned as imperilling the whole state; since styles of music are never disturbed without affecting the most important political institutions."

PLATO, *Republic*.

THE earliest records of Indian music are found in the Rig Veda. The drum, the flute and the lute are mentioned. Instrumental music was performed at certain religious rites; the lute (*vina*) was played at the sacrifice to the *manes*. The existence of several kinds of professional musicians is implied in the Yajur Veda. The chanting of the Sama Veda shows that vocal music was considerably developed.

In later times, references to music in the Sanskrit and Pāli books abound. In the sculptures of Amāravati and Sānchi and the paintings of Ajantā are represented instruments almost identical with those in use at the present day. There are also represented one or two instruments of an Assyrian or Egyptian type, particularly a kind of harp, not now in use.

The prototypes of most or all European instruments in use at the present day are still to be found in the East, the source of the foundations of so much of western culture. The Greeks attributed the greater part of their science of music to India.*

* Strabo, X. III.

Notwithstanding the differences between modern and ancient Hindu music, it is probable that the music of Southern India is more akin to ancient Greek music than any other music remaining in the world. Not only is this the case in respect of structure and theory, but as regards the point of view from which music is regarded. Of the Greeks it has been said, that "inferior to the moderns in the mechanical resources of the art, they had made, it appears, a far finer and closer analysis of its relation to emotional states; with the result that even in music, which we describe as the purest of the arts, congratulating ourselves on its absolute dissociation from all definite intellectual conceptions, the standard of the Greeks was as much ethical as Aesthetic, and the style of music was distinguished and its value appraised, not only by the pleasure to be derived from it, but also by the effect it tended to produce on character." Of this attitude Mr. Dickinson remarks "that moral effects should be attributed to music and to dancing, and that these should be regarded as of such importance as to influence profoundly the whole constitution of a state, will appear to the majority of modern men an unintelligible paradox."* An acquaintance with Indian music would make such conceptions less incomprehensible. The fine and close analysis of the relation of music to emotional states is particularly characteristic; and when we realise the part that music plays in Indian life, how far more inseparably it is bound up with poetry than is the case in the modern West; how it enters equally into the daily life of king and peasant, how it is felt to be the natural expression of all deep emotion and finally how, as explained below, the neglect or decay of Indian music is, as in the case of other arts, inseparably associated with a loss of stability in the economic structure of society,

* G. Lowes Dickinson, 'The Greek view of Life.'

we may believe that Plato spoke advisedly in saying that styles of music are never disturbed without affecting the most important political institutions.

A suggestion made by Lafcadio Hearn respecting Japan, holds good also for India; reading 'Indian' for 'Japanese,' I quote: "to witness the revival of some perished Greek civilisation....were not any more of a privilege than is the opportunity actually afforded to us to-day to study Indian life." I often think it strange that anthropologists and scientists so eagerly investigate the lives and culture of savage peoples, and neglect the great expressions of the human spirit, still remaining in the Eastern civilisations whose character is being changed so rapidly before our eyes. It is, I suppose, a result of the European conviction that while it may be of interest to study others, it were absurd to think that anything could be learnt from them. Europe, indeed, cannot expect to learn much from India so long as she is convinced that her only mission is to teach.

The golden age of Indian music, as of art, belongs to the early middle ages, perhaps from the 5th to the 12th centuries. But in the South, owing to its comparative freedom from the influence of Persian music and from the puritanism of Islam, the science of music was cultivated more nearly in its original forms to a much later time, in some degree even to the present day.

Two causes have adversely affected Indian music in the later middle ages. One of these is the puritanism and intolerance of Islam, by which a serious injury was done to Indian music in the North. One day the minstrels of Delhi paraded through the streets with a bier. Asked by Aurangzib what they meant, they said that Music was dead, and must be buried. "Bury him deep," replied this Calvin of Islam, "that no sound may ever rise from him." But Akbar and Shah Jehan were men of broader culture; the former was himself a musician and composer, the latter is said to have rewarded a famous minstrel with a fee of his weight in gold.

Another cause of the neglect of Indian music has been its association with dancing girls and musicians of low-caste. This in many parts of India has led to an idea that music, like dancing, was not a becoming occupation for other persons, and there has resulted a neglect of its study in the homes of respectable families. Amongst dancing girls however, and by the musicians associated with them, both arts have been maintained in great perfection. A recent puritanical movement known as the 'Anti-nautch' movement has had a reverse influence.

In modern times, more injury has been done to Indian music by the stupidity of educationists, the snobbery of anglicised Indians, and the mechanism of commercial civilisation, than could have been effected by many Aurangzibs. As we have seen, music has been always the delight of Hindu kings.* At their courts were to be found the best musicians. Whatever the luxury or corruption of some Indian courts may at times have been, they were always centres of culture. The place of the royal craftsmen, pandits, astronomers and musicians was assured; their maintenance belonged to the ideal of kingly state. Culture was thus state-endowed, and pursued its way undisturbed by political events. When the Indian courts were done away with, and Indian rulers succeeded by British Governors, all this intellectual and artistic life was undermined.† The English Governor with his efficiency and his reforms, needed no minstrels and no craftsmen;

* Yoga Narendra Malla of Pālam (17th cent.) used on his coins the title Samgitārnnava-Pāraga, "skilled in the sea of music."

† The last Nawab of Lucknow when deposed, brought many musicians and artists with him to Calcutta, where even now some of their descendants remain. The Nawab himself composed a song which is still often heard—*Jab se chora Lakhnan Nagar*, 'Now they have robbed me of Lucknow town.'

all that he needed was a supply of clerks. Compare the state of Tanjore to-day with the evidences of the rule of the Hindu Rajas; the great library neglected, a dead thing not being added to or playing a great part in the growth of national culture; the royal musicians dispersed, and the famous collection of splendidly decorated and ancient musical instruments also scattered; the fine weaving done for the court now forgotten; the training and the emoluments of administrative office in the hands of foreigners to whom the old life and the old culture mean little or nothing,—it is a strange evidence of the greatness of Western Civilisation and the grandeur of British rule in India, that it should so often appear as the destroyer of culture!

Even in Native States the same process is going on; false ideals of economy or efficiency, and a still falser taste have led to the dispersal of the musicians and neglect of Indian music; what does a Maharajah want with the common music that any one can hear, when he can spend hundreds of pounds on gorgeous gramophones and mechanical violins? The Raja of to-day, with his French palaces and his tutor, the Resident, has too often most of the vices, more than the weakness, and little of the dignity of his predecessors. Indian princes might yet do great work for the Indian people, in preserving the national culture; but they have hurried to dispense with it. The king-days are over; it is vain to put ones trust in princes; the national culture must be preserved by the people if it is to be preserved at all. But at present, the lives of the so-called educated, the professional classes in India, are extraordinarily material in their aims, and narrow in their outlook. India, 'progressive India,' does not want art; she wants desperately to be practical. Time will show whether she alone, and for the first time in history, can be or become great with such ideals.

Early Indian music, as explained in the Sanskrit books, appears to have differed much from the modern practice. Its principal feature was a division of the scale into 22 parts called *sruti*, of which four corresponded to a major tone, three to a minor, and two to a semitone. The modern theory, modes and notation are derived from the ancient; but "the whole system has undergone a complete change and gradual refinement, until between the ancient and modern music there exists a difference as clearly marked and perceivable, to even the most casual observer, as that between the modern Anglican chant and the ancient Gregorian tones." *

But there is music still in India. It is not too late to understand this intimate expression of Indian culture. The principal characteristics of modern Indian music are briefly as follows. The octave is divided into 12 semitones, as nearly as possible identical with the notes of European instruments, tuned to equal temperament.† From these twelve semitones, 72 scales or modes (*melakartas*) are formed; of these only 36 are in general use. A *rāga* or melody-type, is a "melodic extension of certain notes of a particular scale or mode, according to certain fixed rules"; the number of *rāgas* is exceedingly large. Each is deemed to correspond to or awaken a particular definite emotion. Almost the only harmony consists in the use of a drone, a continuation of the low or dominant music as in the Scottish bagpipes. The seven notes of the Indian scale are named, in tonic sol-fa wise, *sa*, *ri*, *ga*, *ma*, *pa*, *dha*, *ni*. All that can be written down in this notation is the mere skeleton, or succession of notes proper to the *rāga*. Thus the text of the *rāga* 'Srī' runs :—

* Captain Day, 'Music and Musical Instruments of S. India and the Deccan.'

† *Do.*; but see below.

Ascending mode: sa, ri, ma, pa, ri, sa.
Descending mode: sa, ri, pa, dha, ni, pa, ma, ri, ga, ri, sa.

It will be seen that neither the relative values of the notes, accentuation, tempo, grace notes, or any other details can be thus indicated. These, composing what is called the *murchana* of the *rāga*, can be learnt only by hearing it actually performed, and are in fact so learnt, mainly through the medium of songs in the same *rāga*. There is thus in music that necessary dependence of the disciple upon the master, which is characteristic of every kind of education in India.

I have stated that the 12 semitones of modern Indian music are almost or quite the same as the 12 semitones of Western instruments. But it is said by others that the scale thus employed is a just scale and not the scale of equal temperament necessitated by the use of harmony:* and also that the notes based on a division of the octave into 22 srutis are still employed,† and of this there can be little doubt. It is at least certain that attempts to write down Indian music in staff notation are generally failures.‡ This may be partly due to the survival of the use of quarter and third tones in the essential part of the melody. It is certainly partly due to the fact that the grace notes which play so important a part in Indian music are actually of this character.

A great part of the effect of Indian vocal music depends on the peculiar manner and the skill with which the singer dwells on certain notes, which are varied or trilled,—" vibrating like a bird above the water before it pounces upon its prey "—but not to the extent of a semitone above or below the main note. The same effect (*gamakam*) is produced in

* C. Tirumalayya Naidu, Asiatic Quart. Review, 1904, p. 117.

† A. C. Wilson. 'Short account of the Hindu System of Music.'

‡ But *with the introduction of new signs and conventions*, it is not impossible to write down Indian music in staff notation.

stringed instruments by varying the tension of the string by deflection.

Such effects, so intimately dependent, in the degree and manner of their expression, upon the musician's individual mood and powers, cannot be written down, and so it is that an Indian air, set down upon the staff and picked out note by note on a piano or harmonium* becomes the most thin and jejune sort of music that can be imagined, and many have abandoned in despair all such attempts at record. The music is moreover so personal, and so capable of variation according to the singer's mood, that no record can quite adequately interpret it. The same singer may vary his own rendering from verse to verse, and improvise upon the main theme according to his mood or environment.† It must therefore be understood that the examples given are merely suggestive illustrations, and do not make possible an accurate reproduction of the originals. The only way to adequately study Indian music, is at first hand, by patient discipleship, a practical acquaintance with the instruments, and the help of learned Indians.

All attempts at 'harmonizing' Indian airs, have been, so far, unsuccessful. Whatever the reasons, it has been proved by repeated experience that the natural beauties and national character of the melodies are lost in the process, and the result is something devoid of all the peculiar charm of the original, and lacking in the essential qualities of either Indian or European music. Even the employment of the piano

* Cheap harmoniums are now everywhere common in India.

† Cf: "To avoid misunderstanding, it must be pointed out that by 'a true record of a song' must not be understood one given variation of it, something fixed once for all. The accuracy or correctness of a record applies to most widely-differing variations of one and the same song, and the greater the number of variations, the richer the material for comparative study, the easier it is to find out the most artistic specimen. A comprehensive collection of songs should contain different moments in the development of the same song, both as regards locality and time." E. Lineff, The Peasant Songs of Russia, p. XIV.

or harmonium prove fatal to the delicacy and purity of Indian music, because of the limitation to exact and mechanically limited ranges of notes; and the harmonium especially from its destructive effect upon the quality of the voice and fatal effects on individual taste and refinement.

It is quite likely however, that when sufficient study is given to the matter, harmonisation of Eastern music may be possible. On this point M. Bourgault-Ducondray in his '*Melodies Populaires de Grèce*' writes:—

"We trust that we have been able to show that the application of harmony to Oriental scales is productive of result. Eastern music, till now exclusively melodic, will start upon a new harmonic career; Western harmonic music, hitherto restricted to the exclusive use of two modes, the major and minor, will escape at last from its long confinement. The fruit of this deliverance will be to provide Western musicians with fresh resources of expression, and with colours hitherto unknown to the palate of the musician."

Harmonisation, if possible, with due regard to the preservation of the mode, will similarly add to the resources of the Indian musician.*

The impression conveyed by Indian music is that of a limpid purity of colour effect, and, compared with Western concerted music, suggests a comparison of refined and delicate Indian dyes with the brilliant variety of modern chemical colouring matters, or the flow of a deep river with the rush of a noisy torrent. Western music, apart from emphasis laid upon technique often at the expense of feeling, is complex, troubled, reflecting as it were many sides of life and thought at once. In Indian music the emotions are unmixed, and each in turn exerts its power. Of this sort must have been the music dreamt of by More in his Utopia, which in this respect might have been written of India.

* See 'Music in East and West,' by Maud MacCarthy, *Orpheus*, No. 3, 1908. This article is a valuable comparison of musical ideals and practice in East and West.

"For all their musike bothe that they play upon instrumentes, and that they singe with mannes voyce dothe so resemble and expresse natural affections, the sound of the tune is so applied and made agreable to the things, that whether it bee a prayer, or els a dytty of gladnes, of patience, of trouble, of mourninge, or of anger; the fassion of the melodye dothe so represente the meaning of the thing, that it doth wonderfullye move, stirre, pearce, and enflame the hearers myndes."

(MORE'S UTOPIA.)

A little of the tenderness of Indian music is reflected in a passage from the Arabian Nights already quoted (p. 10). Those who once fall beneath its sway are forever spell-bound by its magic. For the modern world it is too perfect and too refined. It is more the misfortune than the fault of Europeans and Europeanized Indians that they cannot appreciate its beauty. Accustomed to the noisy music of an orchestra, the artificial atmosphere of an upholstered and crowded concert hall, and the complexity and variety of emotion awakened by the elaborate developments of modern Western music, it is not surprising that the delicacy and subjectivity of Indian music leave them little moved, or give only an impression of monotony.

If in comparing the music of East and West, it may be said that in harmony and combined effects the West excels in a field which is almost unknown to the East, there can on the other hand be no doubt that in individual singing, whether technique, expression or subtelty, the East as far exceeds the West. Each has much to learn from, and to admire in, the other.

The Indian singer, as Miss MacCarthy (*loc. cit.*) says,

"seems to concentrate upon his very inmost self in the exercise of his art. His eyes close often in prayerful ecstasy. His pauses are long and frequent. Those who accompany him hang upon his mood and follow its windings without any other support than that of intention. The audience too, must follow as best it can—*he* leads *it*, it does not lead him."

Much of this description is realised in the accompanying reproduction (Plate VI) of an Indian painting (in the collection of the Raja of Satāra), representing the poet Sadi listening to a singer.

Whatever may be gained by possible combination in the future developments of Indian music, the necessity for this intensely personal and rhapsodical singing—so perfect and so natural an expression of the Indian mind—cannot pass away. It were well indeed if room could be found in the West, which, with all its magnificent choral and orchestral development, lacks this lyrical and intensely personal and religious element, for individual expression of the same kind. To some extent, no doubt, the revival of folk-song in England is due to a sense of this need at the present time.

It would be difficult to explain to a foreigner the countless ways in which music in India is bound up with the national culture. It is the resource of India in joy or sorrow. It is a symbol of the immanence of God. "Thou art present even as music in the vina" says a Tamil Poet. It is essential at every festivity, and inseparably connected with all religious ceremonies. "The Vedic chant, composed in the simple Sanskrit spoken three thousand years ago and handed down from generation to generation for more than thirty centuries, ... is to Hindus what plain song is to us. For this ancient chant, like plain song, is bound up with the sacred ceremonials and is wedded to language alike sonorous and dignified. And the place where it is heard, for it is heard only in the temple, is considered so holy, and the strain itself is so simple and devotional, that all who hear it cannot fail to be impressed." The form of the Vedic chants is fixed, and constant throughout India, but this is not the case with other hymns such as those of the Southern Saivites, which are sung to many airs in the homes and temples of the South. Mānikka

Vācagar's hymns are familiar to all and are sung with tears of rapture; there is a saying that 'he whose heart is not melted by the Tiruvāçagam must have a stone for a heart.'

Of dramatic music there is no lack. Certain classical dramas, Rāma Charitam, Arichandra, and the like, are known to the whole people, lettered or illiterate, and appeal equally to both. The South Indian drama is of much importance in the life of the people; just as miracle and mystery plays in the life of Mediaeval Europe. But these representations are now often degraded by the use of cheap harmoniums, called in the South 'Lily-flutes', and by the use of unsuitable and tawdry European scenery and costume, imitations of those tenth-rate travelling companies.

Of special interest are the songs of agriculture and the crafts. By these, I mean all music serving to lighten heavy labour, such as the songs of husbandmen, carters and boatmen; songs embodying technical recipes, and serving as craft mnemonics; songs of invocation of craft or agricultural divinities, or expressing a sacramental conception of a craft; and religious songs,—such as used to be sung at 'spinning bees' in Ceylon before the village weaver's market was "successfully contested" by the products of the wage-slaves of English factory towns. In all these songs music and words are inseparable. The greater part of Eastern literature, popular or otherwise, is written in verse, and verse implies song. Men and women may be illiterate; but when they can recite classical poetry for hours —in language differing at least as much, and in the same way from that in everyday use, as does the language of the Psalms or of Chaucer from the daily speech of an Englishman—then we can hardly deny them 'education.'

Song and agriculture are intimately associated; as you walk along some narrow village track, you may come suddenly upon a hillside clearing where twenty or thirty men are working, and singing at their work, led by an old man with a quavering voice; or a row of stooping women weeding, and singing as they progress steadily across the field in the hot sun, at work in a wet field transplanting rice. Such scenes did not escape the notice of Sinhalese poets; a mediaeval version of the Makhā Deva Jātaka relates that as a certain prince went on his way, he saw "hundreds of girls tending the ear-laden fields, singing sweet songs without fault, wherein his own life was praised." One song relates the exploits of a national hero named Gaja Bāhu. In a well-known reaping song, the *tala* palm is praised.

> In Rayigam Korale renowned there grew a famous *tala*-palm,
> Fairer than speech can tell.
>
> With various beauty crowned,
> From village unto village known;
>
> Fair of hue this palm-flower bloomed,
> Like lotus petals blowing on the tree.

The religious character of many of the agricultural songs is very noteworthy; one sowing song begins as follows.—"When the fields are well prepared, which lie round Balagala-hill, right quickly then the seed is sown by Four Regents of the Earth." A threshing song runs: "This is not our threshing floor, 'tis the Moon-god's threshing floor; this is not our threshing floor, 'tis the Sun-god's threshing floor." Such songs are the fruit of that 'pagan' conception of all life as a sacrament, which gives in the East so much beauty and dignity to common things. What more perfect picture can be imagined of the simple agricultural life of an Indian village, than the bright moonlit threshing-floor, freshly cleaned and consecrated, where the corn is trodden out by the feet of bulls driven round a 'bull-post' in the middle? Even the bulls are in the song.

O bull-king, leader of the team,
O Veriya going next him,
And Kalata the bull-calf,
Make haste to get the threshing done!
I will get your twin horns gilt,
Deck your pair of ears with pearls,
And eke your dew-claws,
So shall I adorn ye!
Ye bulls that wander by the hillside,
Yoked together by a woodbine,
Wearing pearls and coral beads,
And eating tender leaves, . . .
Draw the grain into this threshing floor!

Such are the agricultural songs. Simple as they are, those who have heard them in their own surroundings, will not easily forget them. But even these are less used than formerly, and in a little time will be gone.

Women transplanting rice in the wet fields of Ceylon, sing *jātakas*, and other songs about the Buddha; *Samanala hella* (the song of Adam's Peak); *Padmāvati kathāva*—the loveliest of Sinhalese princesses who became a Rajput bride and *sati*; others, sung by Kandyan women transplanting rice, include a number of *jātakas*.

Music has been thought to have power even over animals and inanimate things. How profound and intimate has been the appeal of Eastern Music to the East, may be guessed from stories of the influence of certain *rāgas* over nature that recall the legends of Orpheus and Apollo.

Indian music can best be heard, and dancing seen, in the great Southern cities such as Madura and Tanjore, and in the native states, Mysore and Travancore. In such places it is still studied as a science by learned Brahmans and patronized by princes. You may engage a dancing girl and her musicians, and invite your friends; seated upon a carpet in a room bare of all furniture, your entertainment is more wonderful than any that money could buy in any other land; more wonderful at least for you, for it is one expression of that national culture of which you too are a part; it is your love and your emotion, your adoration for the Lord which the dancer dances and the singer sings. Another time she is to sing only for you; she brings a *tamburi* or a *vina*, and seated like you upon the ground, pours out for as long as you will, songs of passionate love, or devotion moving you to tears.

Or it may be a man who plays or sings for you; one who has wandered from court to court and received the rewards of princes and kings. He plays the *sārangi* as none else can; the Kashmir shawl he wears is the token of a raja's favour. There are no young men following in his steps; it is well to hear him while you may. In the north he will be perhaps a player on the *taus*, the 'peacock'. He too sings a song of passionate love, something at once so simple and so universal that it includes the love of God and the love of woman; it is part of the method of Indian poetry to carry double meanings, of which each deepens and explains the other, like the shot colours of a double-woven cloth. There are only four of you listening, and to-night you think only of devotion to the Lord, for that thought is in the singer's heart, and he is carried away by his own emotion and neither sees nor thinks of you. And yet if one in his heart thinks only of his beloved on earth, for him too is each love the symbol and revelation of the other.

I am mad for my beloved: they say, what say they? Let them
  say what they will!
Take me for a fool or a mad man; they say, what say they?
  Let them say what they will!
I have nothing to do with them,
  Whether they be pleased with me or angry,
May one only be gracious to me!
  They say, what say they? Let them say what they will!

The Shaikh walks around his sanctuary;
I offer up myself at thy altar,
Call it sanctuary or hovel.
They say, what say they? Let them say what they will!
I have gazed on the glory and sheen of the cheeks of my beloved,
I am burnt up as a moth in the flame,
I am as one drunken:
They say, what say they? Let them say what they will!

So simple is the cry; but it tells alike of the love of those great ones who "are so enchanted with the beauty of the Creator of appearances, that they have nothing to do with the beauty of appearance itself," and of those with whom all the kingdoms of the earth weigh less than a feather in the scale against one woman only, upon whom their heart is set.

Even this is not the most wonderful experience which Indian music holds for those that have ears to hear. There is a music which comes once or twice only to you, and which it is vain to seek. The very greatest of Indian musicians are not professionals, but wandering holy men, players of the *taus* or *sārangi* or *vina*, or singers. Some evening in a northern town such an one passes by your door. You press him eagerly to lodge with you; if he will, to play for you; and he consents. You invite a few friends, and seated on the floor in an upper room, prepare to listen. A brass lamp burns by your side, and all is still. The player chooses an even simpler theme than the last,—"These many days I have not seen thee." He sings and plays, and varies infinitely the expression of this one idea. He becomes almost a part of his instrument, and it and the sound of him. You lose consciousness of things external, and forget to move the wick, which burns dimly and more dimly still. As he plays on—"These many days I have not seen thee," this passionate cry materialises before your eyes as a dancing figure, it may be as the Lord Krishna Himself, it may be as Rādhā, it may be in the form of one beloved on earth, whomsoever your thoughts are set upon, and to whom your love is given. You forget all else, and see only this rhythmic sweet appearance. At last the player ceases, leaving you silent and breathless, and the vision is gone like a dream. What did you see? You ask of one another, and you find that each saw before him his own thought, the one he loved best, and for whom in his heart was lamentation made,—"These many days I have not seen thee."

Perhaps you are in the South. You have gone to a musical party, a wedding at the house of a friend, you are seated with many others on the cotton carpet, and before you is a band of drummers, oboists and players of the *vina* and *tamburi*. A Brahman drums on an earthen pot. A slender girl of fifteen years sits demurely on the floor, dressed in silk brocade and golden chains, her feet and arms bare, and flowers in her hair. Her mother is seated near, back against the wall; she it is that trained the girl, and now she watches her proudly. The only sounds are those of the four strings of the ivory inlaid *tamburi* and the tapping of the drum. As you are waiting for the music to begin, a man with untidy hair and a saffron robe comes in, and your host gives him eager welcome, laying a white cloth on a stool for him to sit upon. All know him well—he is a sannyasi who wanders from temple to temple, preaching little, nor performing many ceremonies, but singing *tevarams* and the hymns of Manikka Vasagar. As he sits silent, all eyes are turned towards him, and conversation drops to a whisper. Presently he sings some hymn of passionate adoration of Siva. His voice is thin but very sweet, melting the heart; his gentle strong personality holds every listener spell-bound, not least the little dancer to whom the words and music are so familiar; he is the dancer's and the drummers' friend and hero as much as yours. Some one asks for a special hymn, 'My God, why hast thou forsaken me?' and he sings.

> Me, meanest one, in mercy mingling Thou didst make
> Thine own,
> Lord of the Bull! Lo, thou'st forsaken me! O Thou
> who wear'st
> Garb of fierce tiger's skin! Abiding Uttarakoça-
> mangai's King!
> Thou of the braided lock! I fainting sink. Our Lord,
> uphold thou me!
> What though I press no more the crimson lips of
> maidens fair,
> With swelling breasts; behold! Thou hast forsaken
> me; though in,
> Not out Thy worthy service, Uttarakoça-mangai's King,
> I am! Thou mad'st false me Thine own, why dost
> Thou leave me now?*

Soon he rises, smiles at the musicians and speaks for a few moments with your host, and so goes away. And then you forget for a time this dreamer, in the beauty of the dance and the clamour of the drums. Of the dance you never weary; there is eternal wonder in the perfect refinement of its grace, and the mental concentration needed to control each muscle so completely; for this is not the passionate posturing born of a passing mood, but the elaborated art of three thousand years, an art that deceives you by its seeming simplicity, but in reality idealizes every passion, human and divine; for it tells of the intensity of Rādhā's love for Krishna. Rādhā was the leader of the herd-girls in Brindaban, and she, more than any, realised the depth and sweetness of the love of Krishna.

Whatever place is held in the heart of Europe by the love of Dante for his Lady Beatrice, of Paolo for Francesca, of Deirdre for Naoisi, is held in India by the love stories of Rāma and Sītā, of Padmāvati and Ratan Sen, and the love of Rādhā

* Adapted from the translation by Dr. Pope.

and Krishna. Most wonderful of these was the love of Rādhā, in the absolute self-surrender of the human soul in her to the Divine in Krishna is summed up all love. In this consecration of humanity there is no place for the distinction—always foreign to Indian thought—of sacred and profane. But when in love the finite is brought into the presence of the infinite, when the consciousness of inner and outer is destroyed in the ecstasy of union with one beloved, the moment of realisation is expressed in Indian poetry, under the symbol of the speech of Rādhā the leader of the Gopis with Krishna the Divine Cowherd. And Krishna is the Lord, Rādhā the soul that strives, in self-surrender, for inseparable oneness. And so both have told of the Lord,—the ascetic, for whom all earthly beauty is a vain thing, and the dancing girl, who is mistress of every art that charms the senses.

The music is to last all night; but you have to be home ere dawn, and as you pass along the road in the bright moonlight, you see that life, and the renunciation of life, lead both to the same goal at last. Both ascetic and musician shall be one Brahman with Himself; it is only a question of time, more, or less, and time, as every one knows, is unreal.

> Oh Lord, look not upon my evil qualities!
> Thy name, O Lord, is same-sightedness,
> Make us both one Brahman.

This Hindu song of Surdas is said to have been sung by a dancing girl at a Rajput court. And there comes to you too the thought, that "Whoso seeth all beings in That One, and That in all, henceforth shall doubt no more."

All this is passing away; when it is gone, men will look back on it with hungry eyes, as some have looked upon the life even of Mediaeval Europe, or of Greece. When civilization has made of life a business, it will be remembered that life was once an art; when culture is the privilege of bookworms, it will be remembered that it was once a part of life itself, not something achieved in stolen moments of relief from the serious business of being an engine-driver, a clerk, or a Governor.

Let those who are still part of such a life take note of it, that they may tell their children of it when it is nothing but a memory. A 'practical' and 'respectable' world has no place for the dreamer and the dancer; they belong to the old Hindu towns where the big temples and the *chatrams* tell of the faith and munificence of kings and merchant princes. In Madras there is the military band, or the music-hall company on tour,—what does it want with ascetics or with dancing girls?

CHAPTER XIV.

Music and Education in India.

"In future years it is to be hoped...that the study of the national music of the country will occupy, as it should, a foremost place in all Indian Schools."

Captain Day, 'Music and Musical Instruments of Southern India,' p. 7.

THE essential error in modern Indian education, as understood by Government, missionaries, and Anglicised Indians, is a refusal or inability to recognize any responsibility to the past. The consequent break in the continuity of the historical tradition is fatal to Indian culture. It is much as if the caretakers of some ancient building, of complex origin, and various ages, hitherto accustomed to make additions and enlargements where and when required, had suddenly abandoned this process of development, in order to pull down the whole building, with the intention of rebuilding it upon a new plan, with the result that most of their energies became occupied with the provision of temporary huts for the inhabitants of the old house thus turned out into the cold. While scarcely any time was thus left for the serious work of reconstruction, and the needs of the day continued to grow faster than ever before, it would not have been surprising if some of the builders and their critics had regretted their haste in abandoning the old building, and reflected that their labours would have been better directed in building a new wing worthy of the old, than in pulling down what already existed. This is in fact just what is happening in India to-day; the destructive rather than constructive character of much of the education given in Indian schools and colleges is being recognized, but so slowly, that it is an open question whether any part of the old structure can be saved, to witness that the ancient builders builded well.

Take music as a single case. The importance of music in education could hardly be over-estimated. "Is not," says Plato, "education in music of the greatest importance, because that the measure and harmony enter in the strongest manner into the inward part of the soul....The man who hath here been educated as he ought, perceives in the quickest manner whatever workmanship is defective, and whatever execution is unhandsome, or whatever productions are of that kind; and being disgusted in a proper manner, he will praise what is beautiful, rejoicing in it and receiving it into his soul, be nourished by it, and become a worthy and good man. Education in music is for the sake of such things as these."

These words a modern Welsh writer does but echo when he says: "Rightly studied, music has all the exactness of pure reason and science, all the expansiveness of the imaginative reason, all the metaphysic of the profoundest philosophy, and all the ethic of the purest religion in it....It is an energy of the mind in the first instance, and is of incalculable advantage in obtaining dominion over the body....Music, properly taught, includes all that is generally conceded to belong to a liberal education."*

These ideas are far more clearly recognizable in Indian than in English culture. But English education, as hitherto imparted and understood in India, has merely ignored the importance of music and art in education. There is in India no educational institution under European guidance where Indian music has any place whatever in the scheme

* D. Frangcon Davies, in 'Wales To-day and To-morrow.' (1907.)

of education. There is no Indian university where Indian music is recognized. Of Europeans engaged in education in India, it is safe to say that not 1% have any knowledge of Indian music as a science, or appreciation of it as an art. The majority frankly regard it as so much noise. This is only one instance, but a typical one, of the unfitness of Englishmen to control Indian education; they are unfitted alike by lack of knowledge and by lack of sympathy. The only place for English teachers in India to-day, whatever it may have been in the past, is in the employ of Indian educationalists, to whom alone they should be responsible. They should be engaged only for special purposes, as in Japan, and should not be allowed to control in matters concerning the aim of method of education as a whole. The control of Indian education is of so much importance that the necessity of gaining this would alone justify the present endeavours to attain political freedom.

Indian girls are often taught to play the piano in English schools, especially in Mission schools.* The only result of this is that they lose the power of appreciating their own melodies; their execution scarcely ever reaches a high level; they cannot afford so expensive an instrument as a good piano in after life; and they despise the inferior taste of their parents and companions at home, who understand Indian music, and for whom European music is meaningless. A writer on Scottish song has remarked, in words most applicable to India: "I have often wondered if the introduction of the cheap piano has anything to do with the decline of song as a means of expression amongst the people. Before

* In many such schools they are taught to sing to a 'baby organ' or harmonium, instruments which, in comparison to Indian instruments, are related much as the steam organ of an English fair is related to the music of Purcell and William Byrd. Few things, too, can be more sad than the waste of faculty involved in the teaching of European scales and songs to children who are capable of using the more elaborate and varied scales of the East.

the era of universal piano playing, the people used to think music; and from thinking to expressing is but a step....now their ambition is to have a piano* and to have their children learn to play. 'Learning music' to them means learning to play the piano, and so that unfortunate instrument has become to them, as to the vast majority, a substitute for music in the brain....many....think it a mark of inferiority to confess acquaintance with their own songs when they can have English music and a piano."†

Music in fact, is contemplated in modern 'English' education in India by no means as an energy of the mind, but essentially as an accomplishment; and it is in the vast majority of cases only as an accomplishment that European music can be taught in India.

The introduction to India of the piano, and Western music generally, is sometimes defended on the plea that both types may be 'enjoyed.'‡ The superficiality of this view is evident;—as if the origin and purpose of music were but 'amusement.' Music and art are not amusements invented by idle men to pass away the time of other idlers; they are expansions of personality, essential to true civilisation, expressions of the human spirit, confirming the sincere conviction that man does not live by bread alone. Music, even more than plastic art, is a function of the higher consciousness. The true musician is the Keltic harper who hears the music of the fairies, or the Indian singer who hears the voices of gandharvas. Only such, like Guṭtila, can call angels down from heaven. I heard of one living singer at Tanjore, who had no voice or power to sing, but longed to express devotion to the Lord in music: he called upon Sarasvati, and like Caedmon, his lips

* In modern India more frequently the cheap harmonium.

† Helen Hopekirk, 'Seventy Scottish Songs,' Boston, 1905.

‡ The word being used in the limited sense of gratification or amusement.

were opened. This true music is as exalted as its source. All great art is truly of supersensuous origin. If art and music are thus expressions, manifestations, it is obvious that the result of imitation and borrowing of the natural modes of expression belonging to other nations whose idiosyncracy and environment are different, must be disastrous; and in point of fact, the attempt to replace Indian by Western music in India, results only in vulgarization, —that essential vulgarization which, as Ruskin remarks, consists in not understanding the effect produced by the imitation.

There may be some whose broad culture enables them truly to appreciate the music evolved by temperaments and in environments so different as those of East and West. There must necessarily be few, and meanwhile the standard of Western music in India is set by those altogether out of touch with it, a bourgeois public satisfied with gramophones. One thing is certain, that a pretence at the same time of despising Indian and of admiring European music is for a true Indian ridiculous. Western culture may be, and will be, of value to the East, but it must be as a post-graduate course—it will not stand in the place of mother milk. We cannot understand others by ceasing to understand ourselves.

Pierre Loti in his book on India, describes the music which he heard in Travancore. The Maharajah's musicians had been playing. "This orchestra," he says, "and these singers belong to the Maharajah....How far away this prince's dreams must be from ours, how different his conceptions of the sorrows that belong to love and death. But this exquisite and rare music of his, reveals to me something of his soul, something that I should never see in our short and formal interviews, burdened with ceremony and foreign words." Now mark the effect of the introduction of European music at such a court; the Raja replaces his group of skilled musicians, whose music even to a stranger is in some measure an interpretation of the national genius, by a newly trained brass band, the performances of which may, with good fortune, rival those of a third rate German band in England. The Raja buys also gorgeous gramophones and a mechanical violin, paying fabulous sums to have them decorated by their English manufacturers. The true artistes of the past he neglects; the hereditary craftsmen, makers of exquisite inlaid and painted lutes and marvellous drums, are left to starve; and to the cultured stranger it can but seem that his must have been an inferior race, with little learning and few traditions worth preserving, for he finds there no new revelation of humanity, only a distorted image of himself.

Quite possibly such a Raja is at the same time 'progressive' and 'enlightened.' He spends money on 'female' education; adopts the Resident's suggestions of founding a museum, or the like, and believes himself to be all that he can or should be. There can be few more depressing sights than that of such men destroying with one hand what they endeavour to build up with the other.

Suppose, for the sake or argument, that one were to admit a superiority of harmony to melody, of European to Indian music. It would be much as if we should say that Greek architecture was superior to Gothic, or *vice-versa*, instead of recognising that each is the expression of a different temperament in relation to different environment and different needs; but let that pass, and ask even on this assumption of superiority what does and must result from an endeavour to introduce European music into India at the cost of Indian.

The comprehension of harmony, especially of its later developments, is even in Europe necessarily confined to those who have had an elaborate musical education, more particularly intellectual than emotional. Only those, moreover, who can afford to pay the cost of expensive concerts, can often hear this highly elaborated music. But in India music is not only for the wealthy virtuoso; it is a part of the national life, it is still an art, not an accomplishment or an intellectual exercise; the music of India is found in the hearts of the people. Rob them of this, by setting up a false standard of 'correctness,' and in a hundred years, how many Indians will have learnt to appreciate elaborate harmonies, or even have the opportunity of hearing European music adequately performed? Probably not one in ten thousand. At the same time, the possibility of creative expression, now common amongst Indian musicians, must die out; for it is not easier to use a foreign musical language than to use a foreign literary speech. So long, in fact, as education is founded upon a foreign culture, you can only produce 'accomplishments' and impart 'useful information'; you cannot give the means of creative self-expression, possible only in the mother-tongue, whether of speech or song.

And if, in a hundred years, some slight acquaintance with European harmonized music should be acquired by a small section of the community, how many will have forgotten in that time the refinement and vitality of their own melodies, and have turned instead to the gramophone and cheap harmonium, or whatever more vulgar mechanical devices may by then have been invented? Almost all will have so forgotten and so turned away, for it is the gramophone and the harmonium, and the cheap ill-taught piano, that stand in India for European music.

It is certain then, that, while the importance of music in education can hardly be over-rated, such education must be primarily an education in Indian music, if it is to have any value as a discipline or as an art, or in any more serious sense than as a mere accomplishment. This is not to say that Indian music must not change or be influenced in any way by changed conditions; but that such change must be organic, not sudden, and that it must be an evolution in accordance with the bent of the national genius. In all education schemes, music must be taken into account as a part of everyday life. Religious songs, songs of agriculture and the crafts, of the love of the land, folk songs must be heard in every school.

In hundreds of Indian schools under more or less direct British control, the only musical education received to-day is the annual singing of a bad translation of the English National Anthem. All this is puerile. The object of education must be to make good Indian citizens, and this can only be effected by using the national culture and the national languages—literary, musical, artistic—as the medium of instruction.

In all these respects, music is but the type of every factor in culture and education. The people's intelligence can be developed primarily only by means of education in the national culture. One must learn to understand that with which they are already familiar before it is possible to understand the unfamiliar, and relate it to one's own life. Only vulgarity can result from imitating what one does not so understand and cannot so relate to one's own individuality. The first necessity in India to-day is National Education.

Music has sometimes been divided into two kinds, folk-music and art music, much as art is sometimes classified into decorative and fine. Both distinctions are half-truths, and sometimes obscure the deeper fact that all art has a fundamental unity. But, accepting the distinction as a temporary convenience, it may be remarked that, in spite of the neglect of Indian art-music in recent times, the

N

folk-music of the people is still everywhere to be heard, and it is only in a living relation to this that a national school of music can be preserved. The attempt to denationalise Indian music by learning European music instead is the sure way to an extinction of the musical faculty, comparable to that which took place in England after the time of Charles I. This decadence coincided with the day when no gentleman's education was considered complete until he had made the 'grand tour' on the continent—and returned from it to turn up his nose, as the Rev. S. Baring Gould remarks, at his old English Manor house, and to call in Italian architects to tear it down and substitute for it a Florentine Palazzo. This is what English-educated and 'England-returned' Indians are doing in India to-day.

As a matter of fact no School of Music has arisen and flourished in Modern Europe that has not been founded on National folk-music, and been concerned with the expression of national aspirations and ideals. Russia may be taken as an example. The founder of the Russian School was Glinka (1803-1857) who was called by List the 'Prophet-Patriarch' of Russian music. He grew up steeped in the folk-music of his own country, and early in life, conceived the idea of composing a national opera. This ambition he eventually satisfied in 'The Life of the Tsar' (1836), an opera which marked an epoch in the musical history of Russia. As Mrs. Newmarch has said: *

'The more thoughtful critics saw that the opera was now in the best sense of the word, and marked a fresh departure in Art—the will of a genuine school of Russian music....He did not merely play with local colour, but recast the primitive speech of the folk-song into a new and polished idiom, so that

* Grove's Mus. Dict. Ed. II., 180-188.

henceforth Russian music was able to take its place among the distinctive schools of Western Europe.'

India may learn from England's experience. From the age of Purcell to the present day, the music of England has been essentially foreign—Italian, German, Russian, Hungarian, but not English. "The question now to be considered" says a writer quoted above "is whether English music is capable of resuscitation. One thing is certain; the present vogue of training English musicians to lisp in the tongue of the foreigner can have no beneficial outcome. It is emphatically not that way that salvation lies."* It was long believed that the English people were actually unmusical, and that there were amongst them no folk-songs, comparable to those of other European nations, the foundation of their schools of national music. This opinion has proved in recent times erroneous; a vast body of English folk-song still exists, and is known to the last generation of country folk, though the present generation is generally scornful of the old songs. It is however, with the true folk-music that the hope of a School of English music rests. The movement for the teaching of folk-music as a part of all educational schemes is growing stronger daily. Its importance has long been recognised in other countries, as Denmark and Hungary.

As Mr. Sharp remarks, the spectacle of a great progressive nation like England, "intent upon the instruction of her people in their own folk-songs," gathered, very often, from the lips of illiterate peasants is a strange one. And yet, if in India we have no more love for our own music than England had in the early nineteenth century, we too must pass through a long epoch of barrenness and formalism, before we awaken to the fact that we have neglected the one thing vital, that is the music

* C. J. Sharp. English Folk Song. 1907.

living in the hearts of peasants, uneducated and illiterate—but more truly Indian than their 'educated' 'superiors'. We too, in time to come, shall be intent upon the instruction of the people in their own folk-songs.* Would it not be wiser to bethink ourselves in time, to save what is with us now, instead of making so needlessly hard the task of those that will come after us, and so needlessly barren our own lives and the lives of those who like some of us have not understood?

These are the days of nation building. Yet how many 'nationalists' are in truth 'denationalists' in their lives and aspirations! They want to be 'free,' to compete with Europe on her own lines, to be 'progressive,' 'advanced,' to gain political power and material success. It is not with these that the future of India lies. It lies in the lives of those who are truly Indian at heart, whose love for India is the love of a lover for his mistress, who believe that India still is (and not merely may be, when duly 'educated') the light of the World, who to-day judge all things by Indian standards, and in whom is manifest the work of the shapers of India from the beginning until now. Without these, there can be no Indian future worth the name. How may they be known? Like answers unto like; but, if an empirical test be asked for, I believe that the love of Indian music and the comprehension of Indian art are tests unfailing.

The direct results of making Indian music an essential part of the educational ideal may be many and various. We have already seen that a proper education in music is everywhere recognized as an invaluable aid in the training of character—the true aim of education. But some aspects of the results

* In speaking of folk-music in India, it must be understood that there is not in India that divorce between folk-music and art-music which, like the distinction between decorative and fine art, is so unfortunate a feature of European culture. The folk-music of India, is the music of all the folk, and really includes the highest forms of 'art'-music.

may be noted in greater detail. There can be no true patriotism without patriotic education. The primary aim of education in India should be the production of Indian citizens. No Indian can be a true citizen of the world, except by being first an Indian citizen, and from that standpoint entering into the life of humanity outside of India. This however is not the time for cosmopolitanism, it is the time when India herself needs Indian citizens; and education in Indian music is an essential part of education in Indian citizenship, whether for those who may never learn a word of English or see even a Raja's brass band, but are more Indian at heart than many of those whose false education has brought so much that is vulgar, so much that is unlovely into the life of modern India, or for those whose life-work leads them into other lands, to bear the message of the East, or to become intellectual parasites, as the case may be. In schools then, Indian folk-music must be taught as a matter of course—religious, agricultural and craft songs, and songs of the love of the land—not forgetting "Bande Mataram." These songs must be orally taught, or to a drum or tambur accompaniment only, not to the piano. To older students the really quite simple theoretical part of Indian music should be taught, as European musical theory is taught in European schools. The result of this education in taste will be that, as the boys and girls grow up, they will be in a position to understand and care for the most highly developed art music of India.

In almost all cases, it will be found that Oriental art, and music and literature have been produced for audiences far more cultivated, in respect of imagination and sympathy, than the audiences appealed to by the artist and musician in the modern West. A great part of this cultivation depended on the existence of a common national culture, in which all shared in the measure of their capacity. The result of this is that the artist in his art relies on his audience to understand refinements and suggestions which now are not understood by reason of the divorce of education from the real life and desires of the people. Hence it is that the 'educated' of to-day have lost their love of Indian music, and find amusement in gramophones. They are no more able to understand real Indian music than the frequenter of London music halls could understand Greek drama. The restoration of Indian folk and art-music to its proper place in Indian education will alter this, and restore the necessary attitude of mind, the preparation, which are required to understand the self expression of India in her music.

How exactly opposite the result at present attained can be, the following episode, only too typical, will illustrate. Not long ago a relation of my own, mother of many children, well educated, and understanding Tamil, some Sanskrit, and English, sang for me certain Tamil and Sanskrit songs. Meanwhile her son, who was then a student at a Government College where his own language, and much more his own music, was ignored and despised, continued to work a gramophone, showing neither any appreciation of the Indian songs, or any respect for mother or guest. If 'civilisation' be the production of, in the best sense, civil persons, how had it failed here! I have met also many who have been ashamed of their own music, even of their own language. The same results may be seen, depending on the same causes, in Scotland and Ireland. Ireland has had the strength to react in time, and renationalise her education, as far as might be in the face of educational authorities quite as unimaginative as those we are familiar with in India. The only hope in India lies in a control of education by Indians.

Another direct result of the present neglect of Indian music in education is what I may call the boycott of Indian musical instrument makers in favour of manufacturers of gramophones and harmoniums. This fact, further elaborated on p. 160, I present to workers in the Swadeshi movement for due consideration in all its ramifications and parallels.

Education in Indian music, that is, education in folk music in elementary schools, will make possible the education of older boys and girls, and young men and women, who possess musical talent, in the art-music of India, song, the *vina*, the *sārangi*. The advantage of these over more mechanical instruments lies in the fact that only the truly musical can master them. A gramophone, and even a piano, often enables the most unmusical person to inflict a suffering audience with his ideas. It is true some efforts have been made by Indians in recent years to provide for education in Indian music, and some of these may be briefly noticed. The Gayan Samaj in Poona and Madras; the Academy of Music in Calcutta, founded by Raja Sir S. M. Tagore, Mus. D. (Oxon.); the Bengal Music School in Calcutta; schools in the central Provinces; individual teachers such as the Ustad of Baroda, court musicians of the Gaekwar, and others: all these by their publications and through their pupils have contributed to the preservation of Indian music. But the influence of even these schools is not always certain. One of the most important is the Gandharva Maha Vidyalaya, or Indian Musical College in Lahore, founded in 1901, for the "revival of ancient Hindu music and its diffusion among the general public." It is a musical college with a variety of courses, extending over periods from six months to two years in extent. The learned principal is assisted by six other pandits. But even here the decline of true Indian music was to be remarked. When I visited the college in 1907, I found 14 boys learning the harmonium, and one only the *vina*, the classical and best instrument of India. One wonders how any college professing to teach *Indian* music can allow a harmonium within its doors. They told me it was so easy,—in three months you can play a tune on it, and earn money at weddings and other entertainments. It is said that the *vina* takes sixty years to learn, and it is hard to find ten more to play it in. Assuredly the harmonium *is* easy, it does not require musical talent, merely a little, very little, perseverance. It is above all easy as played in India; the player attempts no harmonies (wisely perhaps), but picks out a mere succession of notes, the bare skeleton of some Hindustani air, omitting lesser intervals and cadence; or an English music hall ditty. Yes, it is easy. Is not that the secret, or one of the secrets of the degeneration of Indian taste? It is easier to boil your cloth in an aniline dye, than to spend months in producing a beautiful and permanent colour; easier to pick out notes on a harmonium than to play the *vina* or violin; easier to subscribe for shares in a Swadeshi factory than to re-organize and support a village industry; easier to drift than to swim. But for India, is it worth while, is this the Art of Living? Is not an India thus subdued in soul more lost than any India governed by the sword could be?

One cannot gather grapes of thorns; you cannot in the long run get something for nothing. Do not let us pretend that it is possible. If our ideal is one of purely material prosperity, and we have no time for music or the arts, let us have done with them altogether; but if we think that music and the arts belong to the most significant, the most real part of our lives, let us cherish them accordingly. Let us decide; but in either case do not let us pretend that the harmonium and the gramophone are compensations for Indian music. It is not possible for anything to be a compensation for the loss of Indian music.

CHAPTER XV.

Gramophones—and why not?

THE present age is often,—and correctly,—described, as an age of mechanism. For nearly a century, scientific discoveries have been utilised with unprecedented rapidity and success, in making life faster and more comfortable, and in increasing the available sum of concrete knowledge. There are no limits to the possible extension of this process, except in a reaction, of which traces are already recognizable, against the intrusion of the Frankenstein of mechanism upon domains to which he should never have been admitted. For surely mechanism must be for man, not man for mechanism, and man sooner or later will revolt against his own slavery.

Meanwhile, the discovery of each new mechanical device, and of each new method of "conquering nature"—as the stupid phrase runs—is hailed as self-evident proof of progress. With every fresh 'scientific miracle' the self-conceit of a sensation-and-comfort-loving public rises higher.

Yet it is more than possible that later ages will look back upon the present period as one of peculiar blindness in respect of the realities. For a society which sees wealth and progress in things rather than in men must sooner or later stand condemned.

In the present paper I do not intend to treat at any length of the relation of mechanism to industry. It is well to remember, however, that the promise of mechanism has not yet been fulfilled. So far from 'saving labour' for the worker, its chief results have mostly been increased possibility of profit-making for manufacturers, and the replacement of quality by quantity as the means of successful trade. Simultaneously there has been accomplished the degradation of the worker from the level of an intelligent craftsman to that of a living machine. Just how this process works may be illustrated by the following slightly adapted extract from the preface to my 'Mediaeval Sinhalese Art.':—

"Not merely is the workman through division of labour no longer able to make any whole thing, not only is he confined to making small parts of things, but it is impossible for him to improve his position or to win reward for excellence in the craft itself. Under guild conditions it was possible and usual for the apprentice to rise through all grades of knowledge and experience to the position of a master-craftsman. But take any such trade as weaving* under modern conditions by power loom. The operator has no longer to design or weave in and out the threads with his own fingers or to throw the shuttle with his own hand. He is employed, in reality, not as a weaver, but as the tender of a machine...That craft is for him destroyed as a means of culture, and the community has lost one more man's intelligence, for it is obviously futile to attempt to build up by evening classes and free libraries what the whole of a man's work is for ever breaking down. It is no longer possible for culture and refinement to come to the craftsman through his work; they must be won, if won at all, in spite of his work; he must seek them in a brief hour snatched from rest and sleep, at the expense of life itself...There can be no quality of leisure in his work. In short, commercial production absolutely forbids a union of art with labour."

In the words of Ruskin, "Industry without art is Brutality." Yet it should not be thought that the recognition of these facts involves a wholesale attack upon every form of mechanism, or an impossible desire to revert absolutely to mediaeval conditions. Mechanism has come to stay, and has its due purpose to serve as a hewer of wood and drawer of water. But it is for man to see that his

* I have here substituted 'weaving' for the original 'carpet-making', as no carpets are made on power-looms in India at present, and the problem as it concerns weaving is actually before us.

servant does not become his master. That is to say, a discrimination must be made between the legitimate and illegitimate functions of machinery in industry. I do not propose to speak further of this part of the subject here; but this much at least is clear, that the multiplication of unskilled labour which results from the complete subordination of the craftsman to the machine is injurious to the national quality. *Ceteris paribus*, a handicraft is always preferable to a mechanical industry.

The immediate object of this paper, however, is briefly to treat of the relation of mechanism to art, as typified in the relation of the gramophone to music.

Whatever the relation of mechanism to industry, it should be self-evident that it can have no real relation to art. The non-relation of mechanism to art will need no proof to the man who, in Plato's words, "hath here been educated as he ought, and perceives in the quickest manner whatever workmanship is defective, and whatever execution is unhandsome." It is significant, moreover, that it was through education in music that Plato would have attained this very end, that one should, while still young and "before he is able to understand reason," instinctively know what is to be praised and received into the soul, and what is to be despised and rejected. This is the highest understanding, to know without reasoning what is worthy or unworthy. For those who have this understanding, "reasonable proof" is superfluous, and at the same time difficult.

Let us, however, consider the gramophone. It provides, you say, innocent entertainment for all. It will be found that this statement needs considerable qualification. In the first place, to a person of culture---especially musical culture—the sound of a gramophone is not an entertainment, but the refinement of torture. The combination in one person of a highly developed musical taste, and of pleasure in the sound of a gramophone could hardly be imagined. Above all, those who are themselves musicians understand what a blunting of sensibilities is indicated in the acceptance of the gramophone approximation as a substitute for music. The more often and more fully you are pleased and satisfied by this approximation, the more the finer musical sensibilities are dulled. So much for the audience—the effect is to degrade the standard of appreciation.

'Ah, you have never heard a good gramophone,' I am often told. This mythical instrument I never expect to hear. But let us suppose, by way of meeting all possible eventualities,* that a gramophone is available which even a musician cannot distinguish from the real thing. Which is to be desired in a community, the possession of musicians, or of machines that can amuse us? Do we desire men, or things? Every time you accept a gramophone in place of a man you degrade the musician, take from him his living, and injure the group-soul of your people. So it appears that your amusement is not quite so innocent as it appeared.

But to return to the audience—do you really think that the most perfect machine can take the place of a living singer or player? The performance of a musician is never exactly repeated—on each occasion he adapts himself insensibly to the different conditions, and finds also in himself new expression through the old form. There is moreover his personal influence, the power of his personality, the vision of a living man giving expression to emotions in a disciplined traditional art language. For pure hideousness and lifelessness on the other hand few objects could exceed a gramophone. The more

* As a matter of fact, the eventuality considered is really impossible because it is not the principle of the gramophone to reproduce the original sound, but to produce vibrations sufficiently near to the original one to have a similar effect.

decorated it may be, the more its intrinsic ugliness is revealed.*

Again, musical instruments such as a *vina*, *sitar* or *sārangi* have each their own individuality, they possess an individual temperament which the artist must understand and with which he can co-operate. The more such an instrument is played on, the richer it becomes in association, and the more it will be valued by the musician. The manufacture of such instruments is a means of culture to the craftsman; not so the mechanical production of the various parts of a gramophone or harmonium in great factories, where each part is made by a different man, and the whole put together by another.

The intervention of mechanism between the musician and the sound is always, *per se*, disadvantageous. The most perfect music is that of the human voice. The most perfect instruments are those stringed instruments where the musician's hand is always in contact with the string producing the sound, so that every shade of his feeling can be reflected in it. Even the piano is relatively an inferior instrument, and still more the harmonium, which is only second to the gramophone as evidence of the degradation of musical taste in India.

One great disadvantage of mechanical instruments is the fatal facility they afford to the undisciplined and untrained mind to attempt the work of the true musician. A few rupees spent on a gramophone, a few months spent in playing with one finger on a harmonium, and the half educated

* It should be understood that the condemnation of the gramophone here given is concerned solely with its use as a substitute for music as an art. Just as machinery has a due place in industry, so even the gramophone has a use. This use is however as a scientific instrument—not as an interpreter of human emotion. In the recording of songs, the analysis of music for theoretical purposes, and especially, perhaps, in the exact study of an elaborate melody of Indian music, the gramophone has a place. This however is work for the few, and, so far from this use being recognized hitherto, we have had merely the abuse and not the use before us.

philistine of to-day is prepared to dispense with the services of the interpreters of national music, disciplined by years of study and training to the expression of the highest ideals of the race consciousness.

It will be seen that the use of the harmonium is only in a degree less vicious. Easy to learn, it degrades popular taste almost as effectively as the gramophone displaces the trained musician, and destroys the true character of Indian music, and the voice-quality even of the trained musician who makes use of it. These two instruments, if care be not taken, will in a few years more complete the vulgarisation of Indian music.

The highest ideal of nationality is that of service. India, by the scorn which she has cast upon her own arts, by the degradation of standard in her own culture, here sufficiently evidenced by the possibility of finding pleasure in a gramophone or a harmonium, is casting aside this highest privilege of service. Nations are judged not by what they assimilate, but by what they contribute to human culture. India, by her blindness to the beauty that till yesterday was everywhere in and around her in art and music, is forfeiting this privilege of service. For no man of another nation will come to learn of India, if her teachers be gramophones and harmoniums and imitators of European realistic art.